THE LEADER WHO COVERS

Apostle Winston G. Baker

To; Jasmine Dennison
"Mommy"

fr: *[signature]*
12/3/2018

The Leader Who Covers
Copyright ©2017 Winston G. Baker

ISBN 978-1506-905-25-9 PRINT
ISBN 978-1506-905-26-6 EBOOK

LCCN 2017960404

November 2017

Published and Distributed by
First Edition Design Publishing, Inc.
P.O. Box 20217, Sarasota, FL 34276-3217
www.firsteditiondesignpublishing.com

All scriptures quoted are from the King James Version of the Holy Bible.

"A new commandment I give unto you, That ye love one another; as I have loved you, that ye also love one another.

By this shall all men know that ye are my disciples, if ye have love one to another." John 13:34-35.

Foreword

I count it a great honour to write these words as a foreword to this inspiring and insightful book by my brother in Christ Jesus, Apostle Winston Baker. I am particularly blessed by the insights and principles he has, by the inspiration of the Holy Spirit, imparted to the body of Christ and the world through his first book, *Warring Unclean Spirits*.

Apostle Winston Baker is unrelenting in his pursuit of uncompromising servant-hood in obedience to our Lord and Savior Jesus Christ. He graciously ministers to the body of Christ and the hungry souls of men as God has anointed him to operate in several of the gifts of the Spirit with tremendous efficacy and compassion. Apostle Baker is a precious messenger and dynamic ambassador of the gospel of the kingdom of God.

"The Leader Who Covers" is a revelatory treatment of the subject of effective spiritual leadership as God intends it to be practiced. Apostle Baker masterfully outlines the diametric opposition of the satanic kingdom of darkness against the kingdom of Jesus Christ - the Light of the world. Line after line your attention is drawn to the real causes of disunity, confusion and ineffectiveness in our churches and organizations. He directs our attention with relevance and accuracy to the underutilized spiritual forces at our disposal whilst admonishing us to be very careful of the whiles of the devil.

The perspective from which Apostle Baker presents his message is arousing and compelling, inciting leaders and all believers to take another look at leadership that is designed by God to cover His people and expose the works of darkness. As you prayerfully read this timely work you will be inspired to utilize all the tools that have been designed by the Lord of Hosts to destroy every yoke of bondage.

I encourage you to read this manual with an open mind and a ready heart to practice what you will learn. I have been privileged to travel extensively carrying the gospel and I can attest to the reality of the truths embodied by the Apostle in this work.

Prepare to be charged to follow Leaders Who Cover into the glory of the kingdom of God without reservation.

Bishop Dr. Aggrey Scott

Warning!

Satan will be furious if he catches you reading this material as it is being used as a tool to wage war against his kingdom! The bible tells us that "we wrestle not against flesh and blood, but against principalities, against powers, against the rulers of the darkness of this world, and against spiritual wickedness in high places." It is, therefore, imperative that everyone learns how to wage war against the devil and his adversaries. With this said, I feel led to ask the Lord Jesus to cover you under His precious blood:

Prayer:

Eternal and Most High God, I come before you asking that you shield this reader from every satanic attack; I come against every diabolical force and satanic sabotage. I nullify and render powerless, every evil plan or trap in which the enemy would want to place your child. Lord God I pray that you open their spiritual eyes as I bind the spirit of fear now in the name of Jesus!

Father, I thank you for victory! I give you all glory, honour and praise in the name of Jesus.

Amen.

Table of Contents

Introduction

This is a clarion call!

The Lord Jesus Christ has compelled me to release this message to all church leaders and aspiring leaders: Be a leader who covers.

The kingdom of darkness is united and well organized. Unclean spirits do not fight against each other and so the kingdom of darkness is forcefully advancing to the point where crime, violence, witchcraft, sorcery, black magic, necromancy, de Laurence, lodge and other demonic activities have placed our communities, the island of Jamaica and the world at large under siege.

The church appears powerless to engage the enemy in order to take back our children, families, finances, schools and communities. We are by no means powerless because we have been endued with power by our Lord and Saviour, Jesus Christ; but are ineffective because we are divided.

There are many excuses which leaders have given as to why they do not fellowship with other leaders. However, who is right and who is wrong is irrelevant in face of the current predicament which threatens the human race.

It is high time for us to awake from our slumber and recognize who our enemy is. This is a call for us to unite as the body and bride of Jesus Christ, so that we can utilize the 'dunamis' power made available to the church, since Pentecost. As we join forces, we will experience unrivalled revival in our personal lives and churches.

Undoubtedly, this will spread like wild fire throughout our nation and inevitably other regions of the world; sparking the end time revival and restoration so many hearts are yearning for.

'The Leader Who Covers' is a tool meant to bring about repentance, reconciliation, deliverance and restoration; firstly among leaders within the body of Christ and eventually among their congregants.

The word of God details a number of examples of persons who covered leaders and those who did not. The blessings for covering and the consequences for not covering have been recorded for our benefits. I will, according to the leading of the Holy Spirit remind you of these throughout this instrument.

Although this is written with leaders in mind, it is beneficial for every believer within the body of Christ. In actuality, everyone is a leader in one aspect or another; as we lead our own lives and then others. Leadership is necessary in homes, schools, communities, nations and our churches.

I am not a conventional writer or preacher. I remain God's messenger, who writes and speaks as led. This, therefore, is the message from the Lord for this season!

The employment of kingdom language in referring to the people of God in the masculine gender, throughout this book, should not be misinterpreted as a gender bias. All those who have received Christ, are sons of God!

He who has an ear to hear, listen what the Lord is saying to His people now!

Chapter One

Leadership by God's Design

Leadership has a foundation! It was designed by God and is governed by His principles.

It was established for a purpose and it carries an attachment of promises. Before delivering the message God has given me for the body of Christ, it is imperative that God's foundational leadership structure for the church be revisited. In order to do this, we will look at Ephesians 4:8, 11-12 and 1Corinthians 12:28.

> *Wherefore he saith, When He ascended up on high, He led captivity captive, and gave gifts unto men.*
>
> *And He gave some, apostles; and some, prophets; and some, evangelists; and some, pastors and teachers;*
>
> *For the perfecting of the saints, for the work of the ministry, for the edifying of the body of Christ. Ephesians 4:8, 11-12.*
>
> *And God hath set some in the church, first apostles, secondarily prophets, thirdly teachers, after that miracles, then governments, diversities of tongues 1Corinthians 12:28.*

The scriptures mentioned were not intended to initiate a debate as to who is more important in the church. It is to create or recreate a consciousness that God established leadership in the church with purpose and principles. Having done that, He then gave instructions to believers, regarding their behaviour toward leaders.

In Hebrews 13:17, Paul wrote:

> *Obey them that have the rule over you, and submit yourselves: for they watch for your souls, as they that must give account, that they may do it with joy, and not with grief: for that is unprofitable for you.*

Although the scripture references made so far are from the New Testament; leadership originated long before that era. Ezekiel 28:13-17 says:

> *Thou hast been in Eden the garden of God; every precious stone was thy covering, the sardius, topaz, and the diamond, the beryl, the onyx, and the jasper, the sapphire, the emerald, and the carbuncle, and gold: the workmanship of thy tabrets and of thy pipes was prepared in thee in the day that thou wast created,*
>
> *Thou art the anointed cherub that covereth; and I have set thee so: thou wast upon the holy mountain of God; thou hast walked up and down in the midst of the stones of fire.*
>
> *Thou wast perfect in thy ways from the day that thou wast created, till iniquity was found in thee.*
>
> *By the multitude of thy merchandise they have filled the midst of thee with violence, and thou hast sinned: therefore I will cast thee as profane out of the mountain of God: and I will destroy thee, O covering cherub, from the midst of the stones of fire.*

Thine heart was lifted up because of thy beauty, thou hast corrupted thy wisdom by reason of thy brightness: I will cast thee to the ground, I will lay thee before kings, that they may behold thee.

Isaiah 14:12-14 says:

How art thou fallen from heaven, O Lucifer, son of the morning! How art thou cut down to the ground, which didst weaken the nations!

For thou hast said in thine heart, I will ascend into heaven, I will exalt my throne above the stars of God: I will sit also upon the mount of the congregation, in the sides of the north:

I will ascend above the heights of the clouds; I will be like the most High.

From these two accounts, we will agree that leadership was established from the beginning of time. It remains until today and is essential to the advancement of the kingdom of God. In His kingdom we are all children. Regardless of who we are and what we have achieved, we are still children.

As children of God, we are given instructions which God expects us to obey. There are also established principles by which the kingdom of God operates and we are expected to observe them. While God is the ultimate authority in His kingdom, He has assigned leadership roles to persons at various levels within the kingdom. Each individual is expected to know their position, rights and responsibilities and to abide in their calling, thereby maintaining unity within the body of Christ.

Any deviation from God's commands and principles which is left uncorrected, will ultimately lead to division, chaos and anarchy in the church. This kind of malfunction reduces the effectiveness of the church in the society, leading to mayhem.

God is a good God and I love to obey His instructions. I love the fact that there is a blessing in obedience too. In setting the order in the church family and families in general, God gave these commands in Ephesians 6:1-3:

> *Children, obey your parents in the Lord: for this is right.*
> *Honour thy father and mother; which is the first commandment with promise;*
> *That it may be well with thee, and thou mayest live long on the earth.*

The above-mentioned portion of scripture is probably preached in every congregation when our society observes Mother's Day and Father's Day. However, it is equally important for the body of Christ. It is a misconception among many adult believers that they are their own men and women in the church. Many believe that they are too 'big' to submit to spiritual parenting but God calls us 'children'.

God is undisputedly our heavenly Father and those who have begotten us in Christ Jesus through the gospel are our fathers. Paul, in speaking to the brethren in 1Corinthians 4:15-16 said:

> *For though ye have ten thousand instructors in Christ, yet have ye not many fathers: for in Christ Jesus I have begotten you through the gospel.*
> *Wherefore I beseech you, be followers of me.*

He did not leave us to wonder if we were to follow spiritual leaders regardless of the type of life they lead. Before he closed the book, he erased any ambiguity by clarifying his statement in 1 Corinthians 11:1

> *Be ye followers of me, even as I also am of Christ.*

It follows therefore, that as long as we are in the body of Christ, the person on whom the anointing rests which pulled us out of sin, is our spiritual father or mother. This same individual, most times, also is the leader of the local church we become a member of. There are also those instances where persons were baptized for years but went back into a sinful lifestyle. The leader who God anoints to restore that individual to the body of Christ, becomes their spiritual father. Again, if the individual remains as part of that local church, that leader becomes their leader.

The instruction in the word of God to honour your father and mother and to obey your parents in the Lord is without exemption; it applies to all believers. The Lord says that this is right and states the promise that accompanies obedience to this command. Actually the bible took the time to mention that this is the first commandment with a promise.

The promise is clearly stated,

> *"That it may be well with thee, and thou mayest live long on the earth."*

There you have it believers! If you want life to be well; if you want your life to be free from problems, sicknesses and diseases associated with curses, you must learn to honour your parents in the Lord.

If you obey and honour your parents in the Lord, neither will you backslide. You will remain in the body of Christ and fulfill the plans and purpose for which God brought you into the church. Conversely, while we are endowed with the power of choice, there are consequences for disobedience and dishonouring our parents.

Is there anyone who wants to live long? I do! To live long does not refer only to longevity in relation to chronological years, but also to spiritual longevity; so walk with this children; keep this in your belly Christians: God says, "Children obey your parents in the Lord. Honour your father and mother that your days may be long." It will be well with those who honour their leader.

It will be well, because whenever the beasts come to devour the dishonouring children, those who honour their parents and leaders will be protected by God. Whenever the enemy comes in like a flood and the devil sends demons of high blood pressure and diabetes, they will be told, "Wrong Address! Trespassers will be persecuted!" The anointing will declare that this one is covered!

It is well! It is well! It is well! Go ahead and declare it. My days shall be long! I will not be leaving the church. Even after years, I will still be rooted and grounded in the house of God, under the anointing which He placed me. The promise is that the days of those who cover the anointing shall be long. That includes me!

A divine impartation takes place through connection. So, before we embark on the journey to discovering the importance for each of us to be a leader who covers, let us unite, touch and agree in prayer that the Holy Spirit will accomplish the divine will of God for us individually and collectively. We also want to commit to God, any area of leadership and ministry in which we are involved. The ultimate goal here is empowerment to advance the kingdom of Almighty God and experience the blessings which He has promised.

PRAYER:

> *Father, here we are in Your presence, giving You all the glory and honour due unto You.*
>
> *Father please, trust me with Your anointing one more time. Take me behind the veil and reveal that which You desire to impart to us in this season, Oh Mighty God.*
>
> *I ask You in the name of Jesus to speak to Your people; speak to Your children. Please release a rhema word for those desirous to hear from You.*
>
> *Holy Spirit show up in the lives of Your people. Arise Oh Lord and let our enemies be scattered! Give angels*

charge, with swords of fire. Set a spiritual curfew and walk through every area of our lives and ministries.

Father, I come against principalities, diabolical forces and all satanic powers; I render the works of darkness powerless in the name of Jesus. I speak to every contrary wind; I drive them to a far country by the power of Jesus' blood.

Oh God, according to Your word, there are three that bear witness in this earth: the water, the Spirit and the blood. Arise Oh Lord and let Your blood defeat the enemy in Jesus' name.

Oh Lord arise, let the blood of Jesus flow in every area of our lives and ministries. Let the name of Jesus be exalted! Oh God sit upon Your people. Let Your glory saturate our lives. Let the name of Jesus be exalted!

Father we thank You for the victory that flows through Your blood!

We thank You for victory in Jesus' name! Hallelujah!

Chapter Two

Principles and Purpose of Leadership

The very first kingdom principle regarding leadership is that it should be honoured. The purpose of leadership is clearly to cover. God will not entrust a high level of anointing to one who does not display honour for leadership. Never forget this, God will always promote those who know how to give honour to their leaders.

Since we have embarked on this mission to showcase a leader who covers, I suggest that you invest some time in studying the great men and women of God mentioned in the bible. I will highlight a few; but a deeper study will reveal one common characteristic or behavioral trait- they honoured someone. Noteworthy also, is that in return for the honour they bestowed on others, God honoured them.

We can conclude from those evidence therefore, that before God honoured the greats, they first had to honour someone. Show me a successful person and I will show you someone who they honoured. Show me an unsuccessful person and I will show you someone who they dishonoured. God will never release the resurrection power upon an individual who dishonours leadership. Why? The reason is that person reminds Him of the devil.

The scriptures reveal that the devil was chosen by God to be the anointed cherub that covers. What was the devil covering? He was covering the throne of God. This gives rise to another question: Can the devil cover God? Did God need the devil to cover Him? Irrefutably not! Yet God gave him the office to cover Him. So Lucifer was anointed as a leader with responsibility to cover God's throne. He was to ensure that no one brought accusations, disrepute or dishonour to God. If anyone tried to accomplish such evils, it was his responsibility to nullify the attacks.

Now look at this! God is perfect yet Lucifer concocted reasons to accuse Him. Notice that it came out of a heart that was lifted up in pride and covetousness. For that reason, God requires that our hearts be pure in order to enter His presence. Any person with an evil heart will point fingers of accusation at any leader, without fear. God has given us as leaders and members of the body of Christ the same charge He gave Lucifer - be 'a leader who covers'.

Instead of being a leader who covers, Lucifer brought disrepute to the name of God which resulted in his name being changed to the devil. Revelation 12: 9-10 described him as follows:

> *And the great dragon was cast out, that old serpent, called the devil, and Satan, which deceiveth the whole world: he was cast out into the earth, and his angels were cast out with him.*
> *And I heard a loud voice saying in heaven, Now is come salvation, and strength, and the kingdom of our God, and the power of His Christ: for the accuser of our brethren is cast down, which accused them before our God day and night.*

The devil is waging war amongst believers in the body of Christ through accusations. Christians who copy his behaviour are advancing the kingdom of darkness, fighting against the kingdom of God which is undoubtedly reminding God of the devil. Therefore, it behooves each of us to be a leader who covers.

God, who designs leadership within His body is full of surprises. His choice of leadership usually blows men's mind. However, He still reserves and exercises the right to do as He pleases. That makes Him God.

Psalm 75:6-7 would have us to understand this:

> *For promotion cometh neither from the east, nor from the west, nor from the south.*
> *But God is the judge: He putteth down one, and setteth up another.*

When God positions an individual in a particular leadership role, it is often times met with resentment by those who believe that God blundered in the selection process. If this attitude goes unchecked, it opens doors to spirits which dishonour the anointing God placed on His chosen leader.

Only those who are being led by the Holy Spirit will be able to truly appreciate the genius of God in His leadership appointments. He usually selects the most unlikely candidate -by men's standards- to bring glory and honour to His name. It is, therefore, extremely important for us to become knowledgeable of what God expects from us regarding leaders and leadership. This will guide us in developing the right attitudes towards them.

There is a rise in these end times of the manifestation of the five-fold ministry in the Apostolic Church. God is restoring that which was absent for a very long time. We are expected to cover those who God has anointed to do His work and to honour God's anointed and chosen vessels in every area of ministry. To do so will prosper and preserve what God is doing. Revival is here!

To everyone who feels called by God to be an apostle, prophet or prophetess, God says to tell you, "The secret to receiving these gifts is humility." If you are unable to serve a prophet, a prophet's anointing will never rest on you. God would never have given it to Elisha if he had not known how to serve Elijah with humility.

God would never have handed it to Joshua, if Joshua had not served Moses with humility. Jesus would never have bestowed it upon Peter, James and John, if they had not initially served Him. You have to serve with humility and honour your apostle or prophet so that God can pour that which is within Him on you without hesitation.

The Spirit of God in a prophet will impart that which is within him upon those in the body of Christ, as long as they do not possess the spirit of Absalom. The prophet, with joy, will pour himself into these believers as the kingdom of God advances. God's principles emanate from those on whom His anointing rests. Therefore, to honour God, is to honour His principles and to honour His principles, is to honour those on whom He has placed His anointing. This is true, irrespective of your opinion of them.

Any action contrary to the afore-mentioned opens doors to curses in the lives of believers. God is a God of order and never breaks His word. Whenever leaders address these issues in their churches, some are offended. These prophetic utterances are then reduced to mere 'throwing of words and heresies.' But every believer within the body of Christ need not only hear this, but adhere to it. Obedience is what positions believers to receive what God has in store for them in this season!

You should all want to be a part of the move of God in these end times. This message is a clarion call for us to put aside the isms and schisms. It is time to unite! God is repositioning His people to take all that the enemy has stolen from them and forcefully advance His kingdom in the earth realm. The kingdom of darkness is united and organized in unleashing evil attacks against the people of God. The kingdom of God needs to be even more united and strategic in its efforts to defeat the enemy. God has fully equipped us with the five-fold ministry!

The five-fold ministry is the 'hand of God' in the earth. Take a look at your right hand, I will use it to demonstrate the operation of the five-fold ministry.

The thumb or big finger represents the apostle; the index or pointer finger represents the prophet; the middle finger represents the evangelist, who balances the ministry; the ring finger denotes marriage and represents the pastor. He is the loving one in the ministry, like the married person, the pastor focuses on the household of faith; then there is the pinky or baby finger or 'titimus' for the older folks. This finger represents the teachers.

The big finger-the apostle- is the only one whose ministry can touch every other ministry in the kingdom. Go ahead and try this little exercise: check which finger is able to touch all the others easily. The thumb of course! It is the only finger which can swing from one finger to the other with much ease. Likewise, the apostle is the only one who - at the appropriate time- can step into the prophetic ministry; manifest the evangelistic call; operate in the pastoral ministry; and whenever the necessity arises, eloquently impart knowledge as a teacher; all through the power of the Holy Ghost.

This is a high level of knowledge being imparted. However, I believe that for what God is positioning us to do, it is imperative that this becomes common knowledge. Those who God will have to understand this will benefit from it in this season.

This is the ministry that Elisha saw, when he said, "I hear the sound of the abundance of rain." This is the ministry that brings the blessings of God on His people. This is the ministry which releases you from poverty. It is the ministry that brings healing to God's people and brings deliverance from demonic powers.

After Elisha mentioned that he heard the sound of the abundance of rain, he sent his servant Gehazi to look. On returning he reported to Elisha -his spiritual daddy- that he saw nothing. Elisha again sent him to take another look and he returned with the same report. He sent him again and again and in obedience to his leader, Gehazi went each time and brought back a similar report.

However, on the seventh occasion, his report was different. This time he said that he saw a cloud, the size of a fist. That was the hand of God! He received a glance of the church! Hallelujah! Of significance was the fact that it was on visit number seven! Seven! Seven! God said to me, "Son, it was there from the very first time but it was not revealed until the last day." Day number seven, God's perfect day! God's perfect time!

This is the last day! This is the last day! We are living in the last hour of the last day of the church age. Get ready for what God is about to do! God is about to raise you up and use you to defeat the powers of darkness. Can you feel it? Do you have that feeling within your belly that God will raise you up and use you?

God says that you were chosen by Him. As the bride of Christ, God says, "What He has joined together, let no man put asunder." Blessings, He is going to bless you! God wants you to live as the child of a King. "It is not by might; nor by power; but by My Spirit," says the Lord. Don't you just love the Holy Spirit? This is what blows my mind and propels me to love God as much as I do - whenever I see how supernatural He is.

There are times when I am in the presence of the Lord and He transports me from one location to another in the realm of the Spirit. In that new dimension, God reveals things to me which I could not have otherwise known. For that reason, I always crave personal and private time with God. It is a moment for intimacy between God and me. I do not even allow people to hear me whenever I am praying privately.

Prayer is an intimate thing! If you examine the scriptures, they will reveal that during Jesus' time on earth, the apostles did not ask Him to teach them how to heal the sick or cast out devils. Wonder why? Well, as followers of Jesus, they constantly witnessed Him performing those miracles; so they knew from observation, how to have those accomplished.

However, they asked Jesus to teach them how to pray. Why? They had never heard Him pray! Someone is in disbelief, so I will use the scriptures to support this statement. The bible records in Matthew 26:36-46, Mark 14:32-42 and Luke 22:39-46, how Jesus took His disciples to the Mount of Olives at the point of His crucifixion. There, He instructed them to stay at a particular location, while He went to pray; 'a stone's throw away' according to the scriptures. I too have developed the habit of retreating to remote places to pray. Sometimes I am underneath my bed!

I avoid the use of highfalutin speech -big words- in my prayers. I never try to impress God whenever I am praying. Instead, I get real with God! Someone once eavesdropped on my prayer; afterward, he remarked, "Bishop, now I know why you are so powerful. You can certainly pray!"

My ultimate goal when praying is to touch God. I begin at the outer court then move to the inner court. I am reluctant to stop praying until I get behind the veil; right into the Holy of Holies! Prayer is so powerful! It slows down time; it navigates time. Prayer shifts you! It moves you from impossibility to possibility!

Prayer! Prayer! Prayer! Prayer is the key! If you learn how to pray. Prayer makes you an overcomer! Prayer is the arena that graduates overcomers!

Is there anything that have you under pressure?

Is there anything that you want to overcome?

Is there anything that have you in bondage?

Is there anything that is fighting against you?

Prayer! Prayer! Prayer! Prayer is the solution.

At the leading of the Holy Spirit, I opened the doors of the King Jesus Pentecostal Fellowship for twenty one days of prayer and fasting. These twenty one days in the presence of God led to a shift from the natural to the supernatural. If you are so led, you too might want to set yourself aside for a period of time, in the presence of the Lord.

Prayer, fasting, praise, worship, the name, and the precious blood of Jesus are all powerful weapons of warfare. Time spent in the presence of God, guarantees victory in our lives as leaders and believers. We are led by the Holy Ghost and operate in obedience to His commands. We respond positively to instructions given by the Holy Ghost to His children.

For the entire twenty one days of prayer and fasting, believers volunteered to pray in one hour slots. This resulted in prayer being offered twenty four hours daily. The word of God to us was that at the end of the period of prayer and fasting, He would elevate, bless and shift believers. And He did!

Leaders and believers, who love prayer and fasting, can follow as they are led. It is not prudent to make the covenant if you do not intend to keep it. God likes unbroken promises. Pray for yourself, your family, your leader, your church, your community and for the youths in and out of your ministry. Pray also for the deliverance of those who the devil has in bondage.

Ulcer, diabetes, hypertension and menstruation do not excuse you from fasting. God wants to break the shackles holding His people in bondage. In order to be empowered to participate in what God is doing, we must commit to fasting and effectual, fervent prayer. God wants to use these opportunities to usher us and our ministries into the next dimension. Is there anyone ready?

God is bringing back the five-fold ministry in these end times. Leaders, who for years functioned in only two, three or even four areas of ministry, need to recognize the move of God in this season. He is calling leaders to cooperate instead of compete with what He is doing.

Honour ought to be given to those whom God has anointed to minister in each of the five areas as well as the apostle who operates in all areas. All are labourers together with God! There is no need to covet, compete or dishonour! God wants us to position our hearts and spirits in alignment with His words and principles. This is what is necessary for His kingdom to advance forcefully and to overthrow the kingdom of darkness.

There will be those who choose to leave ministries in rebellion. God says, "Let them go!" God says that He will replace them with believers who are willing, committed, respectful and eager to serve in the kingdom - believers who will serve even more efficiently and effectively than those who demitted their offices. No one can boycott God's work! No one at all, at all, at all! Is there anyone saying, "Lord if you are going to use anyone, please use me!"

Some, like Jonah, are determined to find escape routes so as not to fulfill the ministry to which God has called them. God says that the very seat they occupied will no longer be available after they return from their trip to Tarsus.

He that hath an ear to hear let him hear what the Lord is saying today! I know that I am speaking to someone. I just told you about prayer, right where you are, you can make an altar and fix things with God. Hallelujah!

Praise God for what He is doing in these end times! It is important for warriors to pray at all times, especially during the night watches. Most of the warfare in which we are engaged, takes place during the night hours.

Be obedient to the voice of God!

We culminated the twenty one days of twenty four hours of prayer and fasting with an all-night payer meeting as well as praise and worship meeting. Pray without ceasing!

Those who have the opportunity to pray in church, do so. Others can pray at home or work during the lunch hour.

We are all prayer warriors!

Chapter Three

Spirits that Dishonour the Anointing

Throughout this book, you will experience emotional and spiritual turbulence. Although it will sometimes get rough and rugged, I trust you will stay on board. It is necessary to impart these truths to the body of Christ.

The test to determine if your spirit is right and if your heart is pure is to identify the origin of your thoughts and the words you speak concerning a leader. Anyone who boasts of being more powerful and anointed than their leader makes those utterances from demonic influence. I know that's rough and rugged but God is a God of principle and order. He would never place a greater beneath a lesser. Do you understand that?

Elijah was greater while Elisha was in his midst. There will never be two Major Prophets in one ministry at the same time. There will be one major prophet and a number of Minor Prophets. These are anointed to confirm the word of God through the major prophet. Yes! I know that this is deep but it is also important because as leaders and aspiring leaders within the body of Christ, you must know your proper place. If you fail to abide in your calling, you open doors for the enemy to work through you to bring chaos and anarchy in the body of Christ.

You will be used to create division and disruption to the work of God, thus bringing a curse on your life and aborting your purpose and destiny in the kingdom.

The spirit of Absalom at work in a believer, leads them to think of themselves more highly than they ought to think. If you succumb to that plan of the devil, you are in trouble! You are operating in the spirit of error! To make dishonouring and accusatory statements is to show ignorance of the anointing and how it manifests.

Many show scant regard for the anointing God uses to pull them out of sin. Some declare their undying love and commitment to their leader while in the leader's presence and the public's view. However, when given the 'test of honour' they fail miserably. This reveals that they had no genuine regard for the leader, but were rather giving 'lip service'.

Believers are many times not fully aware of the level of anointing which God has placed on a leader in their midst. Sometimes they are ignorant of the high calling on the leader's life and so reject and dishonour him. I have drawn this conclusion by observing the attitude of some believers toward their leaders or spiritual fathers.

I am not addressing leadership in its broadest sense here. I am speaking specifically of those persons whom God chose Himself and anointed for specific purposes for a specific time. When God sent the angel to John-the beloved-who wrote the book of Revelation; John was instructed specifically to write to the angel of the church in Ephesus, Smyrna, Pergamos, Thyatira, Sardis, Philadelphia and Laodicea.

Each church had one messenger; one angel. So it is today, each church has one pastor; one preacher. There are some instances where believers keep moving from congregation to congregation because their leader refuses to stay connected to his source of anointing and his ministry becomes ineffective. To stem this exodus, the leader resorts to constantly engage preachers from other congregations to do what God has called him to do.

Eventually chaos and anarchy develops and believers begin to leave the church, in search of other places where the word of God is being preached, the worship is true and the power of God is being tangibly manifested.

Leaders of the churches to which these believers gravitate must exercise due diligence before receiving these persons as part of their membership. They should be even more cautious about placing them in leadership roles. Whoever walked away from a church in a spirit of rebellion and dishonoured its anointed leadership, will go to another ministry with a spirit to dictate.

These persons leave the church either because they were unable to overthrow an anointed or not being able to dictate how the ministry should operate. They possess a controlling spirit, wanting to direct the leader on how to do that which God has anointed him to do. If their demands are not met, it will be a matter of time before they engage in fault finding and accusations. Eventually they concoct enough stories to give as reasons to leave the church. They then move to another ministry with the same spirit.

An unwise leader or one who is not manifesting the gift of discerning of spirits could readily entertain this spirit of Jezebel and open his ministry to irreparable damage. Sometimes they form alliances with others to annihilate God's anointed vessel because their manipulating attack proved to be futile. All this is in a desperate attempt to control God's servants and undermine leadership to fulfill their personal agendas.

The question to ask is - why did they leave their church if what they are seeking already exist there? I hope I am not being misunderstood here. It is quite possible for God to reposition a believer from one congregation to the other. But I maintain that God is a God of order; a God of peace; a God of principle and is certainly not the author of confusion.

Leaders therefore should imitate Christ when conducting the affairs of the kingdom of God and addressing matters affecting the people

APOSTLE WINSTON G. BAKER

within the body of Christ. Watch for those who aspire for leadership and bring evil report about their previous leader to advance their agenda. If you participate in their dishonouring, exposing and the uncovering of that leader; be sure you will be their next victim of the evil spirit which they carry. It is a spirit that divides. It does not unite!

In Jude, God spoke of those who despise dominion and speak evil of dignities. Whenever you go against the anointing that God has ordained or leadership which God establishes, you are bringing condemnation upon yourself and sometimes your family.

Jude made reference to Michael the archangel. He did not dare to dishonour the devil knowing that God had appointed him as the anointed cherub that covers. Instead of bringing any railing accusations against him, he left him to the Lord. Let the Lord rebuke him.

Of those who dishonour the anointing, Jude says,

> *"But these speak evil of those things which they know not: but what they know naturally as brute beasts, in those things they corrupt themselves* v10.

These are filled up of flesh! They act as though they are powerful and want persons to view them as such. This desire propels them to dishonour God's leadership principles as well as the anointing. They are referred to as 'brute beasts'.

This behaviour opens them to attacks from similar unclean spirits or demons. Demon of depression-beast! Demon of oppression-beast! Demon which form cysts-beast! Demon that result in fibroids-beast! Demon causing disease of the liver-beast! Demon which trouble the kidneys-beast! Demons that walk in your house and set family members at war with each other-beasts! Demons that steal your daughter and put her in the club-beast! Demons that take your son and place him in scamming-beast!

The scripture continues to let us know that in the act of dishonouring leaders, they corrupt themselves. This is followed by a woe; misery. Verse 11 says:

> *Woe unto them! For they have gone in the way of Cain,*
> *and ran greedily after the error of Balaam for reward, and*
> *perished in the gainsaying of Core.*

Woe unto them because they have taken on the spirit of Cain who dishonoured Abel. They have gone after the attitude of Balaam, believing that he had the power to curse the people whom God had already blessed. They perished like Korah, who went up against Moses.

The bible sets forth a number of these as examples for us today. Believers should be wise enough not to repeat their mistakes and suffer similar fate. In this book, I will highlight a few: Lucifer, Cain, Ham, Miriam, Korah, the children with Elisha, King Saul, Absalom, Ahab, Jezebel and Judas.

As in the past, you will notice that wherever authority is established, there is usually someone who the devil enters with a spirit to rise against it. The devil first went against God; Cain then went against Abel; Korah and Miriam went against Moses; Sanballat and Tobiah went against Nehemiah; Saul went against David; Ahab and Jezebel went against Elijah. The list is in-exhaustive!

Jesus - God in flesh came on the scene and He too did not escape these spirits. At the beginning of His three and a half year ministry, He selected twelve followers or disciples. Yet we are told that in such small circle, and among Him who represents the ultimate source of power and authority, was a Judas.

One can more readily understand the devil using the Scribes and Pharisees from the outside since they were clearly opposed to Jesus' ministry. They were operating by the dictates of the religious spirits which consumed them. They were ineffective in their efforts to destroy Jesus and His ministry. However, there was an inside man, who for a mere thirty pieces of silver, offered to get the job done! As with the church today, to betray or 'sell out' Jesus; to dishonour and belittle the anointing, requires an 'insider'.

Regardless of what transpires within the church, it should be taken to the Lord by believers. Depending on the nature of the situation, the matter can also be taken to the relevant person in authority to address same. BE WARNED! Never take the business of the church to persons outside of the church! Never engage in conversations meant to dishonour members of the body of Christ! Cover! Cover! Cover!

If you refuse or neglect to cover the household of faith, your own house will become a living hell! You will begin to think that persons have used witchcraft against you and your family. No obeah is on you! Your enemy dwells on the inside of your mouth-your tongue!

You may be wondering why after being in the church for such a long time, your life is still going around in circles. You begin to say that nothing is happening for you, while others who are relatively new to the faith are experiencing breakthroughs. You wonder if someone has set an evil hand against your life. I am here to tell you that no one has done you any harm. Your curse is self-induced. Check your tongue! The bible says that death and life are in its power. Proverbs 18:21.

The Spirit of Lucifer

Luke 14:11, 18:14, Matthew 23:12

> *For whosoever exalteth himself shall be abased; and he that humbleth himself shall be exalted.*
> James 4:6
> *But He giveth more grace. Wherefore He saith, God resisteth the proud, but giveth grace unto the humble.*
> Proverbs 6:16
> *These six things doth the LORD hate: yea, seven are an abomination unto Him:*

A proud look, a lying tongue, and hands that shed innocent blood,

An heart that deviseth wicked imaginations, feet that be swift in running to mischief,

A false witness that speaketh lies, and he that soweth discord among brethren.

A proud look surpasses being hated by God; in His eyes it is a curse. God hates the behaviour of persons who act as if they are 'big' or important. God pushes away the proud from Himself and draws close to those who are of a humble spirit and knows how to give honour.

One might ask, "What is the cause of so many wars, conflicts and murders?" However, in revisiting the Genesis-the beginning- we see that the first recorded conflict between Cain and Abel was cited in chapter four. A deeper study will reveal that the first war actually occurred long before there was an earth.

Revelation 12:7-8 would have us know:

And there was war in heaven: Michael and his angels fought against the dragon; and the dragon fought and his angels and prevailed not; neither was their place found anymore in heaven.

You ask what? Where? Yes! War in heaven! So, the first war; the first conflict took place in heaven, the dwelling place of the Creator. The question therefore now is: Why shouldn't there be war in the church if there was war in heaven?

This book, as well as my first -'Warring Unclean Spirits'- provides much valuable information on spiritual warfare. However, this publication focuses more in-depth on the spirit of dishonour; it lies at the root of the battles we face. We will now examine the first war more closely. It erupted in the most holy place and exposed the spirit of an archangel by the name of Lucifer.

Lucifer was crowned by God and perfect in his beauty. According to the Holy Scriptures, he was the anointed cherub that covers. He was the angel with portfolio responsibility for worship. Alongside that esteemed position, he was also on assignment to guard the throne of God; that made him a covering cherub. He was there to cover the anointing as he covered the throne of God.

As expected, such responsibilities resulted in him being very influential. He realized however, that all the glory, honour and praise went to the Supreme Being. He observed that all the attention was directed to Jehovah God. All the angels worshipped Jehovah. This drove Lucifer to engage in introspection, after which he began to compare himself with the Almighty. Eventually, he concluded that there is no reason for the glory not to be shared.

His soul searching exercise opened the door to envy and he convinced himself that God was not the only one to be glorified. He considered himself worthy to be a recipient of what was God's alone. The spirit of covetousness led to his desire to be worshipped instead of worshipping God. This desire for attention created desperation which distracted him from his responsibilities. That was problem in the making!

The bible lets us know that pride entered Lucifer's heart. Notice the angel with whom it all began; the one who considered himself powerful and coequal with his Leader; the one who desired to be esteemed above his Leader. He wanted to be like God!

Watch his next move! He resorted to speaking in an accusatory tone in reference to the Most High God. Our minds might experience difficulty in conceptualizing how Lucifer would want to oppose his own Creator, stirring strife and convincing that many angels to worship him in the stead of God. The question arises: What could Lucifer really use to get one third of the stars of heaven to reject their Creator and worship one who was created instead?

This blows my mind, but also gives me consolation whenever my character is attacked by the spirit of Lucifer: God is a perfect God and

Lucifer found fault in Him. When he was through accusing God, a third of the stars of heaven believed and joined him; leading to war in heaven. This helped me to understand why God said,

> *"Woe be unto the inhabiters of the earth and of the sea! For the devil is come down unto you, having great wrath, because he knoweth that he hath but a short time."*
> Revelation 12:12

INFLUENCE! You need to be very careful of influential persons and if influence has been bestowed upon you, be double careful! Be very careful of the people who you respect and the people who you admire whenever they rebel against authority and the anointing. Beware! Lest you be influenced into copying their behaviour.

God does not want us as leaders and aspiring leaders to miss this word! Right now, somebody is in trouble with God and this word that I am about to release will either break you or fall on you! If you truly love God, you will accept the word that He sends to you. If you really love God, you will open your spirit to whatever the Lord has to say to you. If you begin to feel a spirit of rebellion arising within you at this word, then you know that you are in a dangerous position as a believer.

God is asking you this question, "Who did I use to speak into your life when you were in trouble and bondage?" In the moment of desperation; when you had nothing and had no options, you gladly received the word of the Lord through His servant. When the anointing was on his life to release you from that which held you captive, your spirit was quite open and receptive. However, now that you are free and experiencing the blessing of God, a wall has been erected to block you from receiving the word of God from that same vessel.

God wants you to conduct introspection! Ask yourself this question, "What is the difference between then and now?" Check yourself to ascertain what has led to your spirit being closed to the anointed vessel of the Lord. If the anointing of God remains on His servant, then something must be wrong with your spirit! Surely, the spirit of God would not be blocking you from listening and obeying the voice of God.

Believe it or not! This is from the devil! He has somehow crept into your heart and contaminated your spirit similar to how Lucifer contaminated the spirit of one third of the stars of heaven.

Of significance, is the observation that the very first being to rise against the anointing was one also anointed. Be mindful that Lucifer was positioned to cover the anointing; unfortunately, he chose to covet rather than cover. He concocted evil reports about Almighty God, his Creator and used the fabricated stories to gain popularity among the angels.

Nonetheless, there remained another set of angels in heaven who were steadfast in their commitment to honour and serve their Creator only. They refused to open their spirits to Lucifer's devises. They must have strongly rebuked those who sought desperately to corrupt them. These were not gullible; they might have said to those who went along with Lucifer, "Do not bring your evil report to me! I do not want to hear it! I am created and chosen by my God to cover and I will not abandon my assignment."

Lucifer was totally oblivious that his assignment was not an indication of his significance to God but rather a test! Careful thinking would lead one to ask, "What can Lucifer really cover? Can anyone really guard or cover our God, the Almighty Creator of the universe? Can anyone really cover God's throne?" It was a test of loyalty! And Lucifer failed miserably to stand up for the King of all kings!

Let me state emphatically that if God anoints you, He will test you! I restate: If God anoints you, He will test you! He will try you! He will not endow you with a double portion of His anointing that easily! Instead believers move from faith to faith; from level to level and from glory to glory.

God will not pour a certain level of His anointing upon you unless you pass the 'test of honour.' Lucifer failed his 'test of honour' when he dishonoured God and influenced others to imitate his behaviour. He refused to cover the anointing; he did not cover the throne of God. His was the privilege but he opted instead to rebel against God.

Consequently, God decided that such behaviour would not be tolerated in heaven. A line of demarcation was established in response to this question, which rang out across the heavens, "Which side are you on?" This question is being asked within the body of Christ today.

I can only respond for myself. I declare that I am on the Lord's side! What says you? Having declared my position, I further committed within my heart that I will not rise against God's anointed vessels, whether they are in leadership or not. This is not a new resolve but one I made a long time ago: I am on the Lord's side and as for me and my house, we will serve the Lord.

I sense in my spirit that someone is beginning to experience nervousness. Oh yes! You are becoming uneasy because you have dishonoured God's anointing on someone's life. I have news for you! This word is being released for you to make right your wrong. Get back to the straight and narrow! This word is to get you out of 'neutral' and shift you into 'drive'. God is getting ready to switch the body of Christ to a new dimension but some believers are on the wrong side.

This is a clarion call! God is pleading with you and is granting you another opportunity to 'get it right!' You need to sit under the anointing which God has set to cover you and let hell know that you shall not be moved.

For those leaders who are under the attack of the luciferian spirit; declare to all those who hell has assigned against your anointing, that they did not hire you; so they cannot fire you! Sit in the anointing that God has placed upon your life; throw your head back and glorify your God!

The name 'Lucifer' means the light bearer, son of the morning. It means he was the carrier of light; very influential. However, when he took the decision to rise against God, seeking glory for himself, he stepped out of his office. When he went against that which he should have been covering, his light became darkness.

Consequently, Lucifer, who was once full of beauty, now became evil. He, who was the prince of light, became the prince of darkness. He, who once had his dwelling above in the heavens, was now cast down.

Similarly, whenever you turn against the anointing that pulled you out of sin, you are turning to darkness. Lucifer was cast out and was no longer the beautiful cherub that covers. He became the old serpent; that old dragon; the devil. He awaits his ultimate destruction in the lake of fire, which burneth with brimstone in utter darkness.

This was the demise of an anointed one who dishonoured the anointing; one called to cover who instead chose to accuse and expose. Now as an enemy of the anointing, he was removed from his office because pride filled his heart. This is the same pride which manifests today in the body of Christ when believers rise against their leaders, who they are assigned to cover with prayer, fasting and honour.

Satan was cast out of heaven into the earth realm where he has launched a vicious attack against mankind. His aim is to influence us to dishonour God and those He has placed in leadership. That way he can ensure that he and the rebellious angels will not be alone in hell for eternity. His determination is to destroy everything in earth that resembles God; everything and everyone carrying the anointing.

Unfortunately, his influence is far-reaching and his impact is as great among members within the body of Christ, as it is without. This means war! Yes! War in the church! War among the people of God! War among leaders!

Time for a self-check! What spirit are you manifesting? Could it by any chance be the luciferian spirit?

The Spirit of Cain

Subsequent to God creating man and giving him dominion in earth, Satan walked over to the Garden of Eden. There, he wreaked havoc in the lives of Adam and Eve. He was by no means satisfied, so he waited patiently until they procreated and brought sons into the earth. Soon after their first two sons were mature, Satan entered into Cain's heart.

The spirit he placed within Cain was not only to envy, covet and dishonour the anointing but to destroy the vessel which carried the anointing, with the intent that he would stop it from operating in the earth realm. When Cain rose against the anointing in his brother Abel, he murdered him!

The blood of Abel, the anointed of God, cried from the ground. God heard it and enquired of Cain, what had happened to his brother. Most of us are quite familiar with the story and are acquainted with his cold, questioning response, "Am I my brother's keeper?"

Cain died, as we all know, but not the spirit he carried. This spirit has manifested in the lives of mankind throughout all preceding generations. It has since produced many evil spirits with which we wrestle until today. My book 'Warring Unclean Spirits' was written specifically to increase our awareness of a number of the spirits with which we contend today. These evil forces which continue to wreak havoc in our lives all have their root in the spirit of Cain.

I want you to observe closely, the spirits which dishonour and are exposed throughout this book. You will discover that envy is at their roots, so too is covetousness and dishonouring of the anointing. The spirits which seek to murder and totally annihilate an anointed vessel might be referred to by the name of the person in whom it manifested. However, it is in the truest sense, a manifestation of the spirit of Cain.

Without controversy, it is the deadliest of all dishonouring spirits! The spirit of Cain kills! It is the spirit of murder! Its objective is to destroy the one on whom the anointing rests.

The spirit of Cain is that spirit which withholds its best from God but is covetous of those who don't. Whenever God blesses someone who honours Him, the Cain spirit goes into a jealous rage, coveting and envying God's anointed vessel. The rest of this person's time is spent in hot pursuit of that individual with a view to destroying them spiritually and physically.

Individuals with this spirit continuously release evil over the lives of anointed persons, hoping to see evil befall them. Whenever their mission is accomplished and someone backslides and leaves the church to escape the attacks or experience demise - they rejoice.

Like Cain, they are cold and callous; void of brotherly love and affection. That was the same spirit in Absalom and Jezebel. This spirit also manifested in Judas who sent Jesus to the cross.

Self-check! Are there any traits of the spirit of Cain within you? Before you go any further, stop! Get on your knees before God; confess it! Get rid of it! If you don't, the devil will use you to destroy someone whom God has anointed to make a difference in this season. However, if you refuse to heed this warning, remember that you can kill the body but not the soul because the anointing is transferrable!

Cain could not obliterate the plan of God when he murdered his brother Abel. Neither will you! However, like him, your punishment is certain!

Those who are being attacked by the spirit of Cain, should seek God in earnest for direction and protection; remembering always that the battle is the Lord's.

The Spirit of Ham

The devil was relentless in his efforts to destroy the anointing wherever it emerged and manifested in the earth realm. The reason is that whenever the anointing is flowing, God is being honoured and glorified. His ruinous damage in the earth proceeded to Noah's generation.

By this time, God was grieved to the point that He decided to reign judgment upon the entire earth. He placed Noah and his immediate family in the ark which he had instructed him to build. God then unleashed His wrath upon mankind, causing a massive destruction by flood waters. Except Noah's family and those animals that were in the ark, all that remained on the face of the earth were completely wiped out!

We are told that the favour and anointing of God rested on Noah; so in the midst of the chaos, God had preserved a man to bring Him glory in the earth again. God chose Noah to release His anointing in the earth after the flood.

Noah continued to carry the anointing which God placed upon him. Naturally, he aged and needed to pass the anointing to the next generation. He had fathered three sons: Shem, Ham and Japheth. One of whom was to be anointed but like I told you before, the anointing cannot be entrusted to someone that easily; there has to be a test. Yes! The test of honour. No one who fails this test has ever been entrusted with the anointing. It was important for Noah to discover the spirit which his sons carried.

Some believers hate rebuke and there are others who believe that they have the right to rebuke the elder and others whom God has placed in authority. The bible says in Proverbs 13:1:

> *A wise son heareth his father's instruction: but a scorner heareth not rebuke.*

Who are you as a child of God? Do you take rebuke with humility, being desirous of having your spiritual father lead you in the right way?

God loves your soul and whom He loves, He chastens. If so, every now and then as children of God, you will need to get a little whipping to keep on ticking! To resent the whipping is indicative of a rebellious and dishonouring nature. Something is wrong with that spirit. We plea the blood of Jesus against such spirits!

God, at the opportune time, exposed the spirits of Noah's sons to him, so that he could recognize who was worthy to carry the anointing in the successive generation. Noah was enticed by the grapes he had harvested and fermented. He consumed the wine, became drunk and laid naked in his tent.

Oh yes! This was the same man of God who preached for one hundred and twenty years prior to the flood, and made the famous 'Noah's ark' which preserved his family and all that God told him to take in the ark before the flood. God had anointed him and approved him; and yes, he got drunk! So drunk that he laid naked in his tent and had no knowledge of it.

The reaction of his sons to his nakedness was the perfect 'test of honour'. According to the word of God in Genesis 9, when the younger son, Ham, went into the tent and discovered his father's nakedness, he burst into laughter. He saw it as an ideal moment to expose his father and dishonour the anointing. He ran outside the tent to publicly announce what he had discovered in private about his father.

In Jamaican dialect, he might have said, "yuh si seh wi fada nuh so righteous as how im waan wi believe doh?" He was eager to influence the other family members to join him in making a mockery and a public show of his father, thus humiliating him in a moment of weakness.

How many believers within the body of Christ carry the spirit of Ham? Not only searching out the secrets of their leader's life to discover any weaknesses, shortcomings or failures; but with the intent to publicly expose, disgrace, humiliate and dishonour their leader. Like Ham, they want all members of the family of Christ to see their spiritual father as being unholy and unworthy to operate within the position God has placed him.

These are self-righteous folks! Many of whom are being blocked by the spirit of Ham operating in their lives. They are wondering why there is a hold on the advancement of their ministry although they are fasting and praying. God says to let them know that He gave Lucifer the anointing to cover and he messed it up, leading a third of the stars of heaven to do likewise and He will not allow this cycle to repeat itself.

Ham stepped out of the tent, went to his other family members; discriminated against his father and dishonoured the man of God. But there were two other sons, Shem and Japheth. Let me highlight here that God always has a man! Not everyone in the church dishonours and disrespects leaders and God-ordained leadership. There will always be a few who know how to respect a servant of God; a few who know how to pray for their leader.

I sense someone shaking now but I must deliver this word because the spirit of Ham in its full force will still not be able to stop the move of God. However, those who are consumed by this spirit will engender the wrath of God and the curse will therefore extend beyond themselves to their offspring.

As with Ham, generational curses today are sometimes a direct result of God's curse on fore-parents who dishonoured the anointing. The spirit of Ham is easily identifiable in the church. It is a spirit of mockery; a belittling spirit that takes advantage of every opportunity to disgrace others within the body of Christ. This spirit seeks the secret things in believers' lives which it assumes will satisfy the appetite of those who love gossip. It also publicizes anything negative that it discovers in an attempt to expose the weaknesses and failures of others.

The spirit of Ham is a spirit of scandal which assassinates the character of God's people. They go around in the church with the latest 'scoop' on believers. I call them the Apostolic Garbage Collectors; Apostolic Observers and Apostolic Deep Sea Divers. They dig deep into the private lives and past of even new believers to see what they will discover. Their greatest aim is to discredit and disqualify those who are being anointed by God.

This is a soul searching moment! The spirit of Ham cannot hide because it cannot keep its mouth shut and when it speaks, you are able to identify the heart from which the words are flowing. When you speak of someone in the church, including leaders, which spirit are you speaking from or manifesting? This is a self-check!

God is searching for a set of people who will not only resist the temptation to fornicate and to commit adultery but who will also resist the urge to participate in gossiping, tale bearing and backbiting. I plea the blood of Jesus against all forms of insubmission to the principles of God!

Let us return to the story of Noah and Ham to prove how tragic the consequences of uncovering one's leader can be. After Ham disgraced his father, Shem and Japheth -the other brothers- placed their father's priestly robe on their shoulders. They then entered their father's tent backwards and covered him without looking at his nakedness.

Upon regaining soberness, Noah learnt of his ordeal and how his sons responded to his dilemma. He called all three sons to present themselves before him. He began to speak over them and in the process revealed upon whom God had chosen to release His anointing. Even without prior knowledge of this story, you can correctly assume that Ham was completely disqualified.

Ham received something according to Genesis 9:24-25-a curse! And not only on him but on his seed!

> *And Noah awoke from his wine, and knew what his younger son had done unto him.*
> *And he said, Cursed be Canaan; a servant of servants shall he be unto his brethren.*

Imagine that! Ham received a curse on his seed-Canaan! The sad thing was that Noah cursed Canaan, Ham's son and not Ham himself. God honours the words which proceed from those He anoints and so it was that the Canaanites were considered as the vagabonds of the earth. These were the people God dispossessed in order to bring the offspring of Shem into the land flowing with milk and honey-Canaan.

And Canaan begat Sidon his first born, and Heth,
And the Jebusite, and the Amorite, and the Girgasite,
And the Hivite, and the Arkite, and the Sinite,
And the Arvadite, and the Zemarite, and the
Hamathite. Genesis 10:15-18

Those who are familiar with bible history will recall that Ham had another son whom he named Cush. This was the father of Nimrod, the mighty hunter who began the kingdom of Babel, better known to us as Babylon.

Note that this generational curse was not inherited as a result of stealing, murder, adultery, fornication, lusting or lasciviousness. No! It came as a result of Ham's mouth; his disrespectful utterances against his father which was a sign of dishonour for his father's anointing.

You must be careful of the seeds which you allow to fall into the soil of your heart. These seeds, if they are evil, will germinate and change you into an evil person. Be careful of believers within the body of Christ who walk around with syringes of venom. If you allow them, they will inoculate you and before long, you become just as bitter and disrespectful. Dishonouring the anointing is to your detriment and that of your seed, which is your family.

I certainly would not want the spirit of Ham to indwell me! How about you?

The Spirit of Miriam

In the bible, we read of the instruction which God gave the children of Israel about intermarrying. They were strictly instructed not to marry outside of their own people. That needed no explanation; it was clear!

Moses, being the leader of Israel, stepped over this instruction and married an Ethiopian woman-a Cushite. This brought upon him the ire of his sister Miriam, the prophetess. Historians believe that she was the unnamed sister of the baby Moses who was placed on the river in Exodus 2. You will recall how she watched him carefully as he floated on the river, until Pharaoh's daughter found him. At which time, she wisely offered her services to secure a nurse for her baby brother Moses. She used the opportunity to arrange for Moses to be returned into their mother's care. This time she was paid by Pharaoh's daughter to raise her own child.

Moses, -in Numbers 12- now grown, was anointed by God to lead the children of Israel, which included his sister Miriam. Moses' choice of wife was met with disapproval and resentment by Miriam. Maybe her reaction was prompted by familiarity, which we are told, breeds contempt. Miriam went to Aaron, sat with him and dishonoured Moses.

In verse 2, we are told that she asked,

> *"Hath the LORD indeed spoken only by Moses? Hath he not spoken also by us? And the LORD heard it."*

Notice that the person in whose heart the devil places an evil thought against a leader, always seeks to engage others in order to accomplish their mission to destroy or disgrace their leader.

Be careful of those in your midst who walk around with venom in their spirits. They might inject you with that poison and make you their accomplice when dishonouring the anointing. Miriam might have said to Aaron, "Moses should never have done that. He has gone to marry outside of our race."

God wants someone to know that, "If you cannot pray, shut your mouth!" Yes! If you cannot pray for your leader, zip your mouth! Life and death are in the power of the tongue.

Did you realize that the bible referred to Miriam as a prophetess, yet there is no record of her ever prophesying? Let me teach you! Miriam was indeed chosen by God to become a prophetess, but the anointing to prophesy was not yet unlocked within her.

Similarly, within the body of Christ, God has placed ministry in many believers. However, the ministry is not yet unlocked. Before the unlocking, there will be a test! Miriam did not pass the 'test of honour' because she did not know how to honour the anointing that delivered her from Egypt. God chose her to prophesy but in rising against Moses, she reminded God of Lucifer.

I cannot ignore the urge to warn believers, who like Miriam believe that because they share a past with their leader that amounts to some level of familiarity, that they have earned the right to be disrespectful. For every time that a believer rises against his leader, he reminds God of the devil! Do you want a word from the Lord? Well, here you have it: "Do not rise against the leader whose anointing pulled you out of sin and bondage! You will open your life to curses!"

That word was meant to save your soul. God called both Aaron and Miriam to appear before Him. Yet Miriam is the only one cursed. Leprosy fell on her while nothing happened to Aaron. Why? Never touch an office that is higher than yours! God, in His discourse with them, clarified some things while outlaying and reinforcing His kingdom principles regarding leadership.

> *Hear now my words: if there be a prophet among you, I the LORD will make myself known unto him in a vision, and will speak unto him in a dream.*
>
> *My servant Moses is not so, who is faithful in all mine house.*
>
> *With him will I speak mouth to mouth, even apparently, and not in dark speeches; and the similitude of the LORD shall he behold; wherefore then were ye not afraid to speak against my servant Moses?* Numbers 12:6-8.

There was a uniqueness about the relationship between God and Moses, which was not to be found in any other recorded relationships between God and man. Many wonder too, how the King Jesus Pentecostal Fellowship maintains a large congregation and continues to experience such rapid growth despite the evil reports and attacks launched against it.

There is a unique anointing in that house. Believers must therefore, be careful to guard against the spirit of Miriam. Wherever there is a unique anointing, there is a special love! God was letting Miriam know that it would have been different, if she had touched anyone else in Israel but because she touched and spoke against Moses, His anger was kindled against them.

At the departing of the cloud from the tabernacle, Miriam became leprous-white as snow. I will share a revelation here. Do you realize that God in His sovereignty could have dealt with Aaron and Miriam in the presence of the people of Israel? However, even though God was grieved, He privately called and disciplined them.

This again is a profound statement of the nature of God as a Leader who covers. Although Miriam was not spared His wrath, He disciplined her privately and it manifested publicly as a warning to others. This is an important principle by which leaders within the body of Christ must be guided. God, leading by example, covered both Miriam and Aaron while the disciplinary measure was meted out. We need to be like our Daddy!

God's punishment for Miriam serves as a lesson to us that as a direct consequence of dishonouring the anointing, our ministry can be aborted prematurely. God said that Miriam had troubled the camp of Israel. Thank God for His mercies towards Miriam but you might not be so fortunate.

God later hearkened to Moses' cry for mercy on behalf of his sister. He responded favourably and healed her; but only after she completed the stipulated number of days one had to spend in isolation according to the statutes God had laid down for Israel regarding leprosy. This was God's way of dealing with the spirit of Miriam which too reminded Him of Lucifer. He would not allow it to go unpunished so that it could destroy Israel.

If some persons in the church are allowed to continue manifesting the spirit of Miriam without rebuke, they will ultimately tear the church into pieces. They carry a divisive spirit, which not only opposes leadership's decisions, but also conspires against leaders. They are intentional in exposing weaknesses and faults and dishonouring the anointing.

Since Miriam considered herself to be equal to Moses, why did she not deliver them out of Egypt? There are persons, like Miriam in the body of Christ today, who consider themselves equal to or even more powerful than their leaders. Why then did they not deliver or preach the people they are trying to convince of their importance, out of sin or bondage?

Some go out to evangelize, but while on mission, they capitalize on the opportunity to exalt themselves instead of Jesus Christ. Instead of praying for and encouraging those with whom they visit, they belittle and berate their leaders and promote their own agendas. Some spend much time boasting of all the mighty things which they have done, purporting to be the most anointed and most powerful in the church.

The glory and honour that should be given to God, they take for themselves. Does that remind you of anyone? By now, you are beginning to establish the similitude between these dishonouring spirits and Lucifer.

Be wise and learn believers! Be wise and learn!

Throughout the entire bible, the story of Miriam is the only account of God spitting in anyone's face. When Moses asked God to heal Miriam, God said that she must first bear the same reproach that she would have endured, had her earthly father been the one to spit in her face. She was shut out of the camp of Israel for seven days.

My God! Don't let God spit on you! Don't let God spit on you! Do you understand what it is like for God to spit in your face?

If God spits in your face, you become spiritually leprous-your ministry comes to an end. I know that someone is uncomfortable and even scared. I have to share the message that God has given me to release. I know too, that many don't like to hear. However, rather than rebel, let it serve as a warning. Avoid the spirit of Miriam!

God says that you must be careful of the spirit of Miriam! Self-check moment! Ask yourself these questions, "Who am I? Do I cover the anointing or do I expose?" God has called you to cover your pastor, elder, brothers and sisters; from the rostrum to the pew. Cover them with prayer and fasting! God hates those who rise against the anointing.

The Spirit of Korah

A woeful tale is told in Numbers 16 of Korah, who along with Dathan and Abiram rose up against Moses and Aaron. They took two hundred and fifty renowned princes of the assembly and formed an alliance. Korah led the attack on the anointed servants of God, contending that Moses and Aaron had taken too much upon themselves and were acting as if they were the only ones qualified to be used by God.

In Korah's opinion, all the members of the congregation were as holy as Moses and Aaron. He had the audacity to accuse Moses of acting out of order and placing himself as the leader of God's people.

Anyone who is familiar with Moses' story knows that the accusation had absolutely no credibility. On the contrary, Moses struggled to accept this mammoth task to which God had called him; so in response to this attack and dishonouring of the anointing, Moses fell on his face and cried out to the One who called him.

Moses was filled with humility and chose not to defend himself. He told Korah and his followers that the Lord would show them whom He had chosen, appointed and anointed. God would declare Moses' authenticity! Korah went as far as making preparations to take over the priestly duties. He made censers to burn incense and offer sacrifice to God. Can you imagine this level of rebellion, dishonour and outright disrespect for Moses?

The men of the tribe of Levi, who were also involved in the revolt, were actually already chosen by God for ministry. Levi was the priestly tribe. However, they were not content to serve in the office in which God had placed them. They wanted Moses and Aaron's office.

In responding to them, Moses made it plain that it was the Lord against whom they had risen and not him. That is the greatest error made by those who rise against the anointing. In their opinion, whenever they rise against a servant of God's office, they are fighting against the individual who occupies the office. We have observed from all accounts in scripture that they were dead wrong. They were fighting against God Himself. It remains true today!

You will notice too, that God usually fights these battles by Himself. Those who occupy the offices, will often times end up pleading with God for mercy for their offenders. There was so much covetousness and jealousy on display by these men. From all indications, Moses was very hurt emotionally knowing that he had never wronged them.

All two hundred and fifty men, led by Korah came to the door of the tabernacle of the congregation, prepared to take over from Moses. They accused him of incompetence; unable to manage the task to which he had been self-appointed.

The glory of the Lord appeared unto the entire congregation and the Lord instructed Moses and Aaron to separate themselves from their accusers. God's intention was to swiftly consume every one of them. Being a loving servant of God, regardless of the dishonour, Moses fell on his face again pleading to the Lord for mercy on their behalf.

If it seemed unfair that God would have destroyed the entire congregation of the Israelites, instead of only the rebels; what happened thereafter should justify His reason for contemplating such judgment. God who knows the hidden thoughts of men, eventually revealed their true character and intentions. They also rose against Moses and Aaron, alleging that they were the cause of the death of Korah and his allies. These were the same people for whom Moses had just interceded.

Moses said God would confirm whether He sent him and at the end of his speech, the earth opened and swallowed them; not only them, but also their houses and all their goods. They went down alive into the pit and the earth closed upon them. They were completely wiped out of Israel.

Fire then came from the Lord and consumed the two hundred and fifty men who offered incense. God set them as a sign in Israel. The message should be clear: Do not rise against God's ordained leadership! Do not rise against the Lord's anointed! Abide in your calling! The message was plain!

Do you realize how deadly and contagious the spirit of Korah was and still is? Korah and his confederates were all destroyed by God, but the venomous spirit he carried was already injected in a great number of the members of the congregation of the Israelites. Korah had done great damage to the hearts of the people through conspiracy. They were now more rebellious than ever!

Simultaneously, God's anger increased against them because clearly God hates rebellion against Him more than anything else! This was the third time in that chapter that Moses fell on his face, pleading with God for mercy on behalf of the children of Israel. God visited them for the third time in quick succession and His one intention was to wipe them all out because of their dishonour for the anointing!

Moses along with Aaron, made an atonement for the people and the plague stopped. Albeit, an additional fourteen thousand, seven hundred had already met an untimely death.

I deliberately chose not to elaborate on the spirit of Korah because I believe that it is clearly revealed through the aforementioned incident. Certainly, this should serve not only as a reminder but also as a warning to every person in the body of Christ who engages in any such practice.

Self-check! Are you manifesting the spirit of Korah? I plead with you to repent and refrain from those evil, actions immediately! I love you and would never want to witness God's wrath destroying you and your family.

The very thought of this is unbearable! Korah! Korah! Korah! Koraaaaaah! Heed the warning! Do not dishonour the anointing in Jesus' name! I am sure I am speaking to a specific individual! Oh my God, death is at your door Korah! I plead with God for mercy and I plead with you to repent! Korah! Korah! Korah! Do not allow God's wrath to wipe you out!

I wish I could continue to plead with you until you turn but if you don't, your blood will not be on my shoulder. You have been warned!

The Spirit of the Children with Elisha

A very unfortunate tale is told in 2 Kings 2:23-24 of the prophet Elisha and some children:

> *And he went up from thence unto Bethel: and as he was going up by the way, there came forth little children out of the city, and mocked him, and said unto him, Go up, thou bald head.*
>
> *And he turned back and looked on them, and cursed them in the name of the LORD. And there came forth two she bears out of the wood, and tare forty and two children of them.*

Elisha was on his way to Bethel. The word 'Bethel' is derived from two Hebrew words, 'Beth' meaning house and 'El' which means God. On Elisha's way to Bethel, after Elijah was caught up, something strange occurred. The children came out and began to point fingers at the Lord's anointed saying, "Go up you bald head! Go up you bald head." I want you to take keen note of who came out to mock the prophet, the Lord's anointed –little children!

I have to stop and ask these questions: What exactly did they mean by that statement? Where did they get it from?

'Go up you bald head' was a belittling statement which suggested that Elisha was behaving as if he was a prophet but was without power. In other words, he was accused of pretending to be anointed! The children, in saying that his head was bald meant that he had no power; that he was not a true prophet.

This leads me to the second question: Where did they -the children- get that from? I propose to you that they got it from the dining table. They got it as they sat in their homes, overhearing their parents speaking of Elisha. I believe that they were merely repeating conversations they first heard from their parents. Their parents had influenced them to belittle Elisha in saying that he had no power and that he was a false prophet.

This is adequate warning that children too have to be careful of what and who they imitate! The bible instructs children to honour their parents in the Lord. Children, I have a word for you: You need to respect your leaders! You need to respect your parents in the Lord!

These children in Elisha's time disrespected the anointing in rising against Elisha. Would you like to know why? They copied the behaviour of adults who dishonoured the anointing; gathered and spoke evil of the prophet. They considered it pleasurable to repeat all the belittling names and remarks to Elisha. Like their parents, they showed no respect for the anointing.

Now, you might be tempted to ask: "How can this man, being an anointed prophet of God, curse the children? Not only that! He did it in the name of the Lord! So how could a loving God, kill these children?"

Again, I believe that the omniscient God knew that if He had not destroyed them in that stage of their lives, they would have matured into adult haters of the anointing. God in His wisdom made an example of them, certainly to dissuade future generations from such self-destructive behaviour. Who gave them the right to dishonour the anointing, even if they witnessed their parents doing so?

Immediately as Elisha cursed them, two she-bears emerged from the woods. I asked the Lord: Why she-bears? He said, "Son, this was something in the shadow that the church must understand. The bears are beasts of the field and represents demons. In like manner that the children who dishonoured the anointing on Elisha were devoured by the beast of the field; so too will demons wreak havoc in the lives of the children of God who dishonour the anointing today."

For a child of God to rise and begin to disrespect the anointing is for that child of God to open doors in his life through which unclean spirits can enter their homes and ravish it.

This is an opportune time for us to ask God to correct us and set us on a straight path. We are not wise to continue in the error of our ways which ultimately leads to our own physical and spiritual demise. To those who have never indulged in such practices, be warned! Learn from the mistakes of others and avoid a similar pitfall! Pray, "Lord, set me straight and keep me from such evil practices, in Jesus' name."

There are some children with rebellious spirits who are angered by the truth. They are not only rebellious but also hardhearted. Whenever instructions of this nature are given, they get upset; but I am anointed and must speak as the Spirit of God leads. I am anointed and by the grace of God I am committed to speak what He leads me to speak until he brings my service in His kingdom to an end. I am not at liberty to tell you what you want to hear at all, at all, at all!

Neither am I perturbed by those who are offended because I am not desirous of being popular among the masses. The cutting edge anointing which was placed upon me compels me to speak as the Holy Ghost leads, regardless of the consequences.

Some believe that because they speak a few tongues, they have earned the right to disrespect their leaders. Others are convinced that after receiving two visions or have heard the voice of God once or twice, they are qualified to go against the anointing. I am here to warn you! Beware! Lest as children of God, you open yourselves to destruction like the children who dishonoured Elisha-the anointed of the Lord!

The Spirit of Saul

Do you want to hear why Saul died? He died because he was an anointed enemy. There are some anointed enemies within the body of Christ who carry a spirit similar to Saul's. They rise against bishops and other leaders because they want the glory which God has given to His servants.

The reason some church folks speak evil of their leaders is that they crave respect from people and are fooled into thinking that they can achieve that goal by dishonouring their leaders. When Saul heard that the women were singing that he had slain his thousands but David his ten thousands, he became angry.

1 Samuel 18:7 as well as 1 Samuel 29:5-9 inform us that Saul was covetous of the accolades David received as a result of his accomplishments by the power of God at work in him. He began to eye David from that day forward. The reason many are gathered against their bishops is that they have begun to pray for a few people and it allows them to feel powerful. They want to appear as though they are even more powerful than the bishop.

Saul went against the anointed for the same reason. Each time Saul was within close proximity to David, he would reach for his javelin and throw at him, in an effort to pin him to the wall. Similarly, many try to pin their bishops to the wall. Some call their bishop on the cellular phone, aiming to pin him to the wall. Some gather with others behind his back in order to pin him to the wall. When they believe that they will succeed in their venture, they begin to announce his fall, thinking that he will not survive the attack.

They begin to proclaim the collapse of the ministry; the breaking up of the church and the doom of the leader. As a servant of God, this is my response to these naysayers: I have news for Saul; God is the one who called me! I have news for Saul; the anointing is still upon me. I have news for Saul; God is still with me and moreover, He promised never to leave me.

I have this assurance from God, that whenever I go through the waters, He is with me! Whenever I go through the fire, I am not left alone! Whenever I am in the valley, He comes and restores my soul!

Haters, before you blow the trumpet, you need to ascertain whether the bishop still has the anointing! Don't be fooled if he still has the power! As long as the power of God is still on him, he remains the leader and the one whom God has anointed for this season. Don't run ahead of your time! Leaders, echo the blood of Jesus against the spirit of Saul!

God said to me, "Son, every time the anointed enemy throws the javelin at you, just duck! Whenever they lie on you, duck! Whenever they persecute you, duck! Whenever they speak evil of you, duck!"

Leaders, you should do the same. Duck in prayer! Duck in fasting! Duck in the word of God! Some time ago, I 'ducked' into forty days of fasting. On completion, I heard the Lord say, "Three more days." I ducked into that too. Then, on one of my regular trips from Kingston, where the ministry's head office is, I heard the Lord say again, "Son, twenty one more days of fasting."

I felt in my spirit that the Lord was preparing me for wide scale international ministry; United States of America, Canada, England and Belgium were to be reached with the message of the kingdom of God through this ministry. So while others choose to remain in the isms and schisms, I was getting ready for God to take me to another level in the anointing.

The Spirit of Absalom

Absalom dwelt in the king's house. He was born a son of the king's loins; he grew up in the king's house and under the king's influence. The anointing on King David -his father- brought him recognition and gave him the influence he had. Anyone would have thought that this kind of nurturing would create a high level of loyalty and honour for the nurturer. But not so with Absalom, he rose against the anointing.

In order to understand better who Absalom was by nature and character, I will briefly share two other incidents in which he was mentioned before he turned against his own father. In the first incident, 2 Samuel 13 chronicled how he killed Amnon -his own brother- for raping his sister Tamar. Notice that the king was aware of what Amnon did; and although very angry, he did not address the matter.

On the other hand, Absalom not only hated his brother but did not speak to him again for the next two years. He had taken his sister to live with him after she was disgraced. He instructed her to hold her peace and disregard the matter as Amnon was her brother. However, during that time Absalom was carefully plotting the death of his brother in revenge. The well-orchestrated plan was executed; much to the sorrow of King David.

After the murder of Amnon, Absalom fled to Gershur. David mourned for Absalom every day. His heart towards him was revealed in the final verse of the chapter:

> *And the soul of David longed for Absalom: for he was comforted concerning Amnon, seeing he was dead.*

That is genuine love on display!

David's longing for his son was so intense and unbearable that Joab devised a strategy to convince him to send for Absalom. David fulfilled the request of his servant and Absalom returned to his own house. However, David did not allow him to come into his presence.

For the second time, Absalom's true identity was about to be revealed. Two years after he returned to Jerusalem, he decided that he had waited long enough to see his father's face. Twice he sent for Joab, the one who was instrumental in his return to his native land. He wanted Joab to take him before his father. One might have difficulty in believing what he did in order to get his desires met. 2 Samuel 14:30 provides the details:

> *Therefore he said unto his servants, See, Joab's field is near mine, and he hath barley there; go and set it on fire. And Absalom's servants set the field on fire.*

By now an observable trait in Absalom's character is established: Absalom gets whatever he wants by any possible means and at whatever cost! The lives of family and friends are no exemptions. That spirit opens the door to hate, revenge, malice, evil conspiracy, covetousness, murder and the list goes on.

Could this egotistic, self-centered, self-gratifying nature be triggered by the beauty God had bestowed upon him? 2 Samuel 14 describes his physical appearance this way:

> *But in all Israel there was none to be so much praised: from the sole of his foot even to the crown of his head there is no blemish in him.*
> *And when he polled his head, (for it was at every year's end that he polled it: because the hair was heavy on him, therefore he polled it) he weighed the hair of his head at two hundred shekels after the king's weight.*

Clearly, he was accustomed to being in the limelight and was determined to have it remain that way.

Having that background reference on Absalom, it becomes easier to see how he could make his own father the next person on his hit list. He now wanted the throne and his father occupied it! Absalom strategically positioned himself at the gate to Jerusalem and carefully set the launching pad for his next conquest.

> *And it came to pass after this, that Absalom prepared him chariots and horses, and fifty men to run before him.*
>
> *And Absalom rose up early and stood beside the way of the gate: and it was so, that when any man that had a controversy came to the king for judgment, then Absalom called unto him, and said, Of what city art thou? And he said, Thy servant is of one of the tribes of Israel.*
>
> ***And Absalom said unto him, See thy matter are good and right; but there is no man deputed of the king to hear thee.***
>
> ***Absalom said moreover, Oh that I were made judge in the land, that every man which hath any suit or cause might come unto me, and I would do him justice!***
>
> *And it was so, that when any man came nigh to him to do obeisance, he put fort his hand, and took him, and kissed him.*
>
> ***And on this manner did Absalom to all Israel that came to the king for judgment: so Absalom stole the hearts of the men of Israel.***
>
> *And it came to pass after forty years, that Absalom said unto the king, I pray thee, let me go and pay my vow, which I have vowed unto the Lord, in Hebron.*
>
> *For thy servant vowed a vow while I abode at Geshur in Syria, saying, If the LORD shall bring me again indeed to Jerusalem, then I will serve the LORD.*
>
> *And the king said unto him, Go in peace. So he arose, and went to Hebron.*

> *But Absalom sent spies throughout all the tribes of Israel, saying, As soon as ye hear the sound of the trumpet, then ye shall say, Absalom reigneth in Hebron.*
> 2 Samuel 15:1-10.

Imagine that! The spirit of Absalom sat in wait two years perfecting his plan to murder his brother in revenge; sat two years awaiting the opportunity to get back in his father's palace and presence: sat forty years turning the heart of the Israelites from King David, his father, to himself. He had now become a callous murderer! His own father, the anointed of God, King David was now his next target.

His tactics to gain the love and confidence of the people involved belittling, berating and dishonouring his father whilst exalting himself. He highly recommended himself as the most suitable person to rule over Israel; possessing the perfect leadership style and qualities to satisfy the needs of Israel. He convincingly demonstrated his love, affection and concern for them by the constant attention he gave them.

All this was happening while the king was consumed with the affairs of Israel and pouring so much love on an undeserving Absalom. It is not surprising that God said that David was a man after His own heart. Can you imagine, David loving Absalom so purely and deeply that when he should be punishing him for his wrongdoing, he was crying daily for him for over four years?

My heart sank within me as a father, both in the natural and spiritual, when I observed the spirit of Absalom in operation and how David responded in each situation. When David saw Absalom for the first time, he was so consumed with love for his son that he embraced and kissed him. He was totally oblivious that all the love, affection and mercy he had shown Absalom, could not hinder the Absalom spirit from making him his next victim.

It is hard to conceive that a spirit like this existed and even harder to believe that this is one of the main spirits at work within the Apostolic church today. I have also come to realize that confronting this spirit is as difficult for leaders whom God has called and anointed today as it was for David in those days.

Through Absalom's political campaign, he exposed all the weaknesses and failures in his father's leadership and personal life. As part of his conspiracy to overthrow David, Absalom constantly assassinated his character, convincing the people that the king did not care for them. He appealed to the emotions of the people through expressions of sympathy and empathy. He led them to believe that he was feeling their pain and desperately wanted an opportunity to alleviate same. Then he so cunningly made his appeal to their desire for someone to be in leadership who would give them the attention that he had devoted himself to give daily. He purported that he was the man!

If I had not had my own share of experiences and also witnessed this onslaught on the lives and ministry of other leaders within the body of Christ, I would probably wonder if this callousness could exist among born again believers. I hate to be the one to confirm that the report is evil but true. Absalom succeeded in stealing the hearts of the people from David to himself.

As leaders and aspirant leaders within the body of Christ, we must be very careful of the spirit of Absalom. The Absalom spirit plots, schemes and conspires to overthrow anointed leadership. An individual who possesses this spirit will pretend to be able to accomplish things that the leader who God has anointed is unable to.

Absalom's speech was convincingly sweet; his mouth was oily! This spirit will tell you just what you want to hear. This is a spirit that manifests through self-exaltation; while presenting himself as the solution to the people's problems, his ulterior motive was self-gratification.

Believers with itchy ears and who desire man's approval rather than God's, are prime targets for the Absalom spirit. Believers who desire a word from God, which is not forthcoming within their scheduled time, are open and quite vulnerable to this spirit. They need to understand that the leader who God anoints is unable to function without the unction of the Holy Spirit. These anointed leaders are therefore not at liberty to tell you what you want to hear at the time you want to hear it. An anointed leader is led by the Spirit of God and must please God rather than man. This usually makes them unpopular among those who are always in need of a word. But it makes one carrying the Absalom spirit very attractive to them.

Now, I have a word from God! He says to tell the believers that whenever there is a word from Him, He wants His people to open their spirit and be receptive to that word. God says that there is an Absalom spirit that will walk fearlessly into your home; it will walk into your business place; it will walk into your organization; and yes, right into your ministry! It strikes with an aim to destroy anointed leadership and establish itself in its place.

This Absalom spirit is extremely influential, subtle and conniving. It sets out to expose any weakness in a leader by running ahead to perform any task in which the leader is delinquent. The Absalom spirit goes after the hearts of the people, convincing them that he should be in charge. He dishonours the anointing and leads the people to question the authority of the one whom God has placed as the head. Those deceived by this spirit will also dishonour leaders, discrediting the anointing of the leader and exalting themselves as being equally or more anointed.

Whenever this spirit is manifesting in the church, persons in the congregation are targeted. The Absalom spirit bypasses the leader and goes to members with messages that they claim to have received from God. The message might be for the individual, for another individual, for the leader or for the church. They sometimes enter homes and business places, offering prayers, counselling and solutions to problems which believers face.

In the process, they engage in discussions about other believers, the church and the leader. On the surface they appear genuine but their intention is really to seduce God's people and to appear equally or more powerful than their leader. Thank God for the Holy Spirit and the gift of discerning of spirits which exposes them to the believers with pure hearts.

This spirit at work within the body of Christ operates the way Absalom did in Israel. They gather and share information with sweet words in order to increase their importance and popularity among the brethren. In the end they sow discord, create division and dishonour the leader God anoints so that they can take over his office or ministry.

There are some common statements among persons who carry the Absalom spirit:

Has bishop visited and prayed for you since you have been sick?
The Lord has given me a word for you.
The Lord has shown me your problem.
The Lord gave me a word for the church.
The Lord showed me that such a person is not living right.
Did you call the bishop?
Did the bishop return your call?
I heard this, did you hear about it?
The Lord used me to do this.
I got this vision.
I got this dream.
I see the church splitting.
I see the ministry closing down.
The leader should never have done that.
This is what the leader should be doing.
God says He is going to use me to do this and that.

This is the office that the Lord says He has given me but the leader cannot see, hence the reason I am not placed in it. The list goes on.

At the end of the onslaught of the spirit of Absalom on the leaders and the body of Christ, some lose the desire to remain under the leadership which God placed them. Others believe they don't need the leader's prayer, godly or fatherly advice anymore. Ultimately, their admiration shifts from the leader God gave them to the one whom the enemy used to convince them he is the most efficient one to lead.

Absalom, how can you? I question. Don't you realize that it was the anointing of your father that covered you and made you into who you are? You knew nothing about prayer; you knew nothing about prophecy. What you are seeking to do in your leader's stead are all the gifts which you observed him manifesting under the anointing. It is the anointing on his life that has brought you to where you are currently.

Absalom, how can you use your influence to seek to overthrow your father, when it is his love and mercies towards you that kept you alive? Have you forgot as a father, how he nurtured, protected and succored you?

For all the hell you have been through, if it was not for the anointing on the leader God gave you, you would have been insane or your bones white. Have you so soon forgot how your spiritual leader prayed and fasted for you and attended to your emotional, spiritual and physical needs? How then can you conspire to dethrone him?

The Spirit of Jezebel

God called a man by the name of Elijah and commissioned him to prophesy. In the process of fulfilling his mandate, the devil rose Jezebel against the anointing. Jezebel was determined that not one prophet should live! She launched her attack against Elijah to silence him.

God used Jehu to slay Jezebel and preserve the anointed one! Thank God that for every Jezebel, God has a Jehu.

The spirit of Jezebel is the spirit that seeks to silence the anointing and the anointed one through murder.

As a means of further equipping you with both knowledge of the spirit of Jezebel and how to war this unclean spirit, I recommend that you read chapter seven in my first book, 'Warring Unclean Spirits'.

The Spirit of Judas

To sell out Jesus required an insider to team with the enemy. Judas, driven by his love for money, was open to the enemy to get the job done. He turned out to be very instrumental in Jesus' crucifixion, being used by the devil to betray Jesus for a measly thirty pieces of silver.

Be careful that the devil does not find any opening to make a Judas out of you! He will use you to sell out the anointing. In today's society, believers 'sell out' the anointing with just a phone call; one Facebook post; one text message; one video clip; one newspaper article; one gossip and the list goes on. It is mind boggling to see some of the things even believers put on social media in order to increase followings, gain popularity among the masses or just for the hype.

The ease, with which we reach the world now, greatly increases their reach to persons not just locally but overseas. They team up with these persons against leadership and the anointing. Many churches and church leaders have suffered at the hands of these Judases.

If you want God to use you or to raise you up, do not betray your leaders; brethren, the anointing or the body of Christ with your unsaved relatives and friends. Don't sell out the church with your unsaved coworkers! Don't sell out the church with your boss! Remember that even the weakest saint was purchased by the efficacious blood of Jesus Christ and is therefore precious in God's sight.

Don't sell out the church! Don't be a Judas!

The reason some believers' children backslide and none of their relatives will attend church is based on the manner in which they dishonour the church leaders and members in their presence. They consume them like a well prepared meal at the dining table at breakfast, lunch, dinner and anytime in between! These trusting family members lose every desire to fellowship with the believers whose characters were defamed at the dining table.

No one is spared from these vicious attacks - not the bishop, elder, choristers, youth leaders, deacons, ushers, missionaries or evangelists. Absolutely no one is spared! They devour from the pulpit to the pew! Eventually, the devil succeeds in releasing an evil spirit through these believers on their family members, making them resentful of their fellow brethren in the Lord and rebellious against church.

They conclude that the church is filled with hypocrites and they no longer have an interest in hearing the word of God being ministered. By the actions of their Christian family members, a wall is now erected between the unsaved family members and the church. This hinders them from entering the presence of God. They will be lost if God does not intervene but for sure their blood will be on your shoulder. God will definitely hold you guilty! You killed your loved ones because you refused to cover!

Only a Judas does these things. These things need not be in the body of Christ and must be destroyed. Judas would certainly want us to believe that he is a friend of Jesus, being one of His twelve followers. Yet Judas' friends were the very folks-the Pharisees- who were determined to kill Jesus. The platform for betrayal was now perfectly set with a kiss.

Many Christians fail to recognize the importance of having wisdom. God is a God of wisdom, who calls us as fools but admonishes in James 1:5 that

> *if any of you lack wisdom, let him ask of God, that giveth to all men liberally, and upbraideth not; and it shall be given him.*

You cannot be real if you carry a Judas spirit. A person, who genuinely loves someone, will never be caught speaking evil of the person who they profess to love. Neither will their friends be the enemies of that individual. Love covers! Shake that spirit of Judas off!

Choose rather to honour and be real! If you are not with the leader, you are not with the leader! Don't play both sides; that is hypocrisy! It may sound strange but I had to say it because it is a necessary truth. There is too much pretense and hypocrisy within the body of Christ.

It is time to be real! Get rid of the isms and schisms so that the hand of God can do mighty things in our midst and the name of God be glorified. We need to be honest because the hatred that we try so hard to disguise from man is actually wide open to God. Unless we rid ourselves of it, after a while it will be exposed to our fellowman.

Believers must beware and use wisdom in dealing with those who have been identified with the spirit of Judas. This is good advice: Feed Judas but never eat from him. I am teaching you wisdom! This is a reality which needs to be taught in the church.

Judas will take poison from your enemies and place it in your food. I know it is getting tough! But you need to be wise as a child of God. *Wisdom*, the bible says in Proverbs 4:7,

> *is the principal thing. Therefore get wisdom: and with all thy getting get understanding.*

The Lord Jesus said in Luke 16:8

> *that the children of this world are in their generation wiser than the children of light.* Jesus also says that, *No man can serve two masters: for either he will hate the one, and love the other; or else he will hold to the one, and despise the other.*

You therefore must be able to identify the spirit of Judas operating in your life and environment.

The Spirit of Delilah

The spirit of Delilah is similar to the spirit of Judas. Delilah and Samson were friends at the same time that Delilah was friends with the Philistines. They quickly capitalized on this connection and offered her money for the secret of Samson's strength. Sure enough, she sold him out!

I have learnt not to trust anyone who is closely associated with those that I am knowledgeable of who hate and seek for opportunities to destroy me. There are some persons one could never approach with an evil report about their leaders or brethren. They will never show interest in what you are saying. If you persist in trying to contaminate their spirit against their leader, you will eventually get a sharp rebuke.

Shut up! Or Zip up! This is the message that God wants to get into someone's spirit today. God wants it to get to the very bottom of your belly; there it should be so bitter that it results in a nauseous feeling. You need to vomit all the poison, the venom which has been deposited into your spirit against the anointing.

Which side are you on? Genuine friendships are not affected by what a person wears or where a person resides. It is a matter of the heart! If you respect someone, it will be a respect that is shown both in their presence as well as their absence. You should not be afraid to identify with the individual wherever you go and in whatever condition he is. Their physical appearance should never alter their loyalty to you.

Some are challenged to accept a leader with my personality. Some have preference for leaders who are attracted to members employed in high positions, drive prestigious vehicles and are influential in society. They are only proud of their pastor if he associates with those in privileged circles.

Sorry, I do not 'fit the bill!' You do not need to be in any of those positions for me to consider you a friend. I am interested in identifying with those with a pure heart, irrespective of their background or position in life. As a matter of fact, I cannot forget where God has taken me from! And the truth is, I do not consider myself as an accomplished individual because all that I am today, is what God has made me to be.

Nobody has to remind me to remain humble! I cannot help being attracted to those who truly love God and the anointing. I surround myself with those who strive to please God; those who cover the anointing and desire in earnest to see the manifest glory of the risen Lord.

No one is perfect! Even those who truly love the Lord err from time to time. Some are quick to spread evil report against believers who transgress. By the grace of God, I will not allow their venom to poison my spirit against my weak brethren. I will not sell them out to the enemy! As a leader, a servant and a child of God, I am committed to guarding and covering the anointing.

Whenever one under my leadership is in error, I will prayerfully address the situation in the most appropriate manner and as the Spirit of God leads. I am aware of the fact that believers ought to receive rebuke and correction. It is therefore, important for believers to do what the Lord and their local church require. However, in the meantime I will cover the anointing on that person's life.

I love the anointing and I live to cover it! Reassure someone today that you are covering their anointing, their gifts, their ministry and their calling. Let someone know today that you are committed to covering them! Hallelujah!

You should be able to declare boldly, "I love you and God does too!"

If you are reading this book and you are not saved or as a Christian, you are manifesting any of the spirits I have exposed, I invite you to pause at this juncture and make things right with God. God is inviting you to surrender your life to Him and get baptized in Jesus' name, if you have not yet done so.

If you have not yet received the baptism of the Holy Ghost, the anointing is present right there with you for you to be filled. Receive the Holy Ghost! It is already given so go ahead and receive it and praise

God for this precious gift. The Holy Ghost brings the anointing in and on you, equipping you to cover others in the same way that God positions others to cover you.

Now, you are at the right place, at the right time for your break-through!

Chapter Four

Spirits that Cover the Anointing

Covering the anointing is a choice!

For every opportunity that presents itself for you to go against your leader, you should make the choice to cover your leader instead. Don't be an accuser! Refrain from pointing fingers at your brothers and sisters. God says, "I did not call you to accuse; I called you to cover." It is so important for us to receive that word in our spirit so that God can use us to bring deliverance to His people.

For that reason, God usually takes the one who is last; discriminated against and exposed and places him first. The least becomes the greatest and the greatest becomes the least. Why? God resists those who consider themselves to be something; He resists the proud and draws near to the humble.

Whenever you begin to consider yourself as 'Miss This' or 'Mr. That' and see yourself as being a powerful prophet or prophetess; just remember that in God's eyes you are really nothing at all, at all, at all! I think I need to reemphasize that! Whenever you think that you are something, you are really nothing at all! At all! At all!

On the contrary, those on whom you debase and speak of as nothing; in reality, are the ones who God considers great; so for each time you put me down, God raises me up. When you say that God cannot use me; is when He will show that you are dead wrong! That is the time that He will display His awesome power through me.

Ministry is in you! God wants to destroy every curse hindering the manifestation of His power in the lives of His people. God will deliver you and raise you up as a testimony of the great mercy, grace, healing, and resurrection power of our Lord Jesus Christ.

We do not indulge in the use of oils, powders or candles. We do not "read-up!" That is the spirit of divination in operation. We demonstrate the raw, undiluted power of Jesus' blood. Prophecy and word of knowledge are just two of the nine gifts which God has given to the church. These gifts enable us to live the victorious life ordained for us before the foundation of the earth.

Extend your faith in God and watch Him heal and deliver. In the presence of this power, the anointing covers us and drives out every unclean spirit opposing our blessings and prosperity. All this is available through the power in the name of Jesus and the rich, red, efficacious blood of Jesus.

You need to cover yourselves, your loved ones, your friends and families with the blood of Jesus. Anytime the enemy sees the blood, he has to pass over you. God wants to use the church as a witness that He delivers. He wants to anoint us to demonstrate His power to set the captives free. There is an anointing to heal the sick, raise the dead and set captives free. God also anoints one to be the captain - the leader in each house.

In raising up an army, God always selects a captain and for the army to secure victory in battle, it is imperative that all warriors learn to honour their captain. Those unable to honour their earthly captains will not be able to bestow honour on the Chief of Command in heaven. You must first display honour for the under shepherd before displaying honour for the Shepherd of our souls. The biblical principle established by God is that you must honour what is visible to be able to honour the invisible.

Thereafter, you can stretch forth your hands towards the sick and experience the fire of God flowing through those hands to burn out every sickness and disease and bring healing to God's children. The manifestation of the power is wrapped up in your obedience to God's words.

Then with authority you can declare healing. You can speak to anything affecting God's people and command it to go by the power of Jesus. You have the authority to drive it to a far country in the name of Jesus! You have the power to command that God's people be completely healed in the name of Jesus.

You can confidently declare like Peter, "Silver and gold have I none but such as I have, give I thee. In the name of Jesus Christ of Nazareth, be healed, be delivered and be set free NOW!" Hallelujah! Anoint the head of God's people and cover them from those who launch attacks against their lives. Cover them by echoing the blood of Jesus! The blood of Jesus delivers! It breaks witchcraft and all manner of curses in Jesus' name.

We cast out unclean spirits so that people can be filled with the Holy Spirit and power. In the presence of Almighty God, surgeries are cancelled and God is declared as the healer of His people. That is what God has called us to do! The battle is not yours; the battle is the Lord's. All the praise and glory goes to Him! We are anointed as leaders to cover and serve the people of God.

In the event that any evil report brought against a leader has a foundation, the leader who covers should wisely respond to the accuser. It is the responsibility of the leader who covers to cover the accused leader. Cover him in prayer, fasting and by whatever other means the Spirit of God will direct.

Galatians 6:1 says,

"Brethren, if a man be overtaken in a fault, ye which are spiritual, restore such an one in the spirit of meekness; considering thyself, lest thou also be tempted."

It is never right for a leader within the body of Christ to speak evil of another leader! NEVER!!!

Be careful that you never become so desperate to have your church filled with members that you resort to compromising the word of God to attract people to your ministry. Be on the double watch for the spirit of Ham! Resist it! Do not embrace it! Do not join Ham in making a mockery of God's anointed or seek to benefit from someone else's weakness or nakedness! Cover it!

Did you hear me? Cover! Cover! Cover! Be a leader who covers!

I have had a number of persons both locally and overseas, expressing the desire to become partners with me in ministry or to receive leadership roles in King Jesus Pentecostal Fellowship. However, I am very prayerful about these situations and have even encouraged some to reconcile their differences. After all, we are a part of one body!

Let us face it, if a renowned member of a congregation who is in a high leadership position, for example an assistant pastor, evangelist or elder, leaves a church to seek membership within another church in close proximity; undoubtedly, people will begin to probe to discover what is wrong. Cover! Cover! Cover! Cover!

I believe it is imperative that leaders remain in prayer and fasting so that God can reveal the spirits of prospective and active members. We need to rely on the Spirit of God to give us clarity and direction in these matters. Suffice it to say, God will not send someone to another ministry to dictate to the leader He has anointed and appointed there. If He sends you to a new leader who is being led by Him, you are there to sit and learn!

TEST! TEST! TEST! God will never give you a double portion of His anointing, if you do not go through the 'test of honour' and come out as pure gold. I sat under the tutelage of the bishop who I consider the greatest teacher in Western Jamaica for years. I can state without fear of being refuted, that no one can come forward and truthfully say that I, Winston George Baker, have ever spoken evil of the man of God.

I have learnt not to touch the Lord's anointed! I know that if I wanted to, I could; because there is no perfect person on the face of this earth. None is perfect! Not one! If I should begin to search for faults, without fail, I would find; but this little boy has learnt one thing: Never speak evil of God's anointed! God says:

> *Touch not Mine anointed, and do My prophets no harm.*
> 1 Chronicles 16:22 and Psalm 105:15

Anyone who desires for God to raise them up needs to first know the office or ministry to which they are called and abide in that calling. Your office is given to cover the anointing and not to expose. Cover! Cover! Cover! Be a leader who covers!

I was chosen! What about you? If you know that God chose, anointed and appointed you, declare it! I was chosen to be a leader who covers!

If you believe it is the will of the Lord for you to venture into your own area of ministry, my advice is that you 'LEAVE WELL!' That was God's instruction to me when I was about to leave my training ground and become the under-shepherd of the King Jesus Pentecostal Fellowship. When I began ministering in that church, it had eight members, five of whom were active.

At the point of receiving the instruction from God, I was so scared! I plunged into prayer and fasting, just to be sure. The Lord confirmed His directive for me to leave and guided me through the process. He instructed me to write a letter, expressing my gratitude and informing the leader of His will for my life and ministry at that point. I was further instructed to give a month's notice in order to facilitate a smooth transition by allowing adequate time for a suitable replacement to be identified.

The Lord also told me that during this period, I should continue to serve as usual and not to make any announcement of my pending departure. During my tenure, I had baptized four hundred persons and I continued to serve as I was led. At the appointed time, I left with my children only. Although many from the church I had left eventually became members of the King Jesus Pentecostal Fellowship, it was their personal decision to remain under the anointing which God used to deliver them. I never enquired how many came or how many remained.

This was a time of character formation in me and I give the Lord Jesus Christ thanks for it. The Lord saw it fit to assign me responsibility in a different area of the vineyard. I am humbled and remain at His feet for direction.

An important part of my mandate is forthcoming in this book. I want to pass on to all leaders, and aspiring leaders that which God has taught me over the years; before training, during training and after placing me on this newest assignment.

Have I arrived? Most certainly not! As a young leader in a rapidly growing ministry, I can identify with Moses. If God goes with me, I will go! Thank God that with each new challenge, He multiplies grace and courage. I can also identify with Solomon. My prayer on a daily basis is that He imparts the wisdom, knowledge and understanding which is necessary for me to accomplish His bidding. The ultimate goal is to bring glory and honour to His name.

I have learnt to cover not compromise!

The Spirit of Michael the Archangel

The bible says that Moses was dead and a new door was about to open. God instructed the angel Michael to take the body of Moses and put it to rest in a quiet place where no demon could find it. Michael did as he was instructed and the devil came to him, demanding that he disclosed the location of Moses' body.

As expected, he employed intimidatory tactics. He may have said, "Hey Michael! Do you realize that I am still anointed? Haven't you noticed that I am still powerful?" Whatever strategy he might have employed would definitely display his cunning craftiness. The devil is indeed a cunning fellow.

You might be familiar with this little song which is very popular among Sunday school students: "The devil is a sly old fox, if I could catch him; I'd lock him in a box; lock that box and throw away the key, for all those tricks he played on me.

He sure is playing tricks in the church today! In like manner, he wants believers to dishonour the anointing. He tried to initiate a 'word war', intending for Michael to respond in a manner which amounted to dishonouring the anointing. If Michael had surrendered to the devil's scheme, he would then accuse him before God.

Michael, the arch angel was however, conscious of whom Satan was -the anointed cherub that covers- so he refused to dishonour the devil because he was aware of the importance of not going against an office that is higher than his. Michael did not engage the devil in war. That would have spelt trouble!

Lucifer was next to God. As I told you before, he was the anointed cherub that covered the throne. He had hoped to get Michael on his side by tempting him to dishonour the anointing; but Michael, like some believers today, responded in wisdom.

> *Yet Michael the archangel,*
> *when contending with the devil, he disputed about the*
> *body of Moses, durst not bring against him a railing*
> *accusation, but said, The Lord rebuke thee.* Jude verse 9

Notice that Michael did not rebuke the devil. No! He decided to leave the devil to the Lord; let the Lord rebuke him. This behaviour is quite the opposite of many believers within the body of Christ today. Some believers today are of the view that they have the right; the power and authority to put the bishop and other leaders 'in their place'. They have no fear to rebuke anyone in authority who they assume to be walking contrarily.

With the far reaching effect of technology today, the social media has become a very popular place where believers 'bash' their bishops and other leaders within the body of Christ. Instead of using the media as communication channels to advance the kingdom of God, many believers use it to dishonour God's anointed vessels. There are too many times to mention, where even church leaders use this powerful tool to expose, instead of cover other leaders within the body of Christ.

Do not be confused now! A believer should never compromise or be partaker of other believers' sins. I am not advocating here that you condone the wrongs of others; but there are principles within the word of God, stipulating how these situations are to be addressed. If we choose to disobey the word of God by dishonouring our leaders, we are invoking the wrath of God on our lives as well as that of our descendants.

Although I am addressing leadership issues within the body of Christ, that which I have imparted on the evils of dishonouring leaders, is also applicable to the home, school, community and wider society. As children, we bring curses on ourselves whenever we dishonour our parents. As students we bring curses upon ourselves whenever we dishonour teachers. As employees, we invite all manner of ills in our lives whenever we dishonour employers. As citizens of any country, we open ourselves to destruction and the wrath of God when we dishonour our leaders; political and otherwise.

I will reiterate, if you cannot speak well of someone, keep your mouth closed! Those who know how to pray, do so! Those who know how to fast, do so! The effectual fervent prayer of a righteous man availeth much. Always remember:

PRAYER IS POWERFUL!
LOVE COVERS A MULTITUDE OF SINS!

JUDGE NOT!
CONDEMN NOT!

Notice that Michael did not have the right to rebuke Satan even after he was cast out of heaven. So who are you to dishonour those on whom God has chosen to place His anointing? Some go beyond all boundaries the moment they experience the anointing once or twice; speak in tongues and get a vision or two. But wisdom is on display if we follow the example recorded in Jude by Michael.

You should do the same! Say, "I won't rebuke you for the Lord will deal with you in due season." Yes! Leave them to the Lord! This is a message for all real warriors in the kingdom of God. You must be aware of the nature of the warfare in which you are engaged and allow Jesus Christ, your Commander in Chief to give the instructions on how to engage the enemy in combat. You need to know when to leave the battle to the Lord. If your response to any attack involves going against God's ordained leadership, DO NOTHING, BUT FAST AND PRAY! SAY NOTHING BUT GOOD!

Verse eight of Jude speaks also of those filthy dreamers who defile the flesh, despise dominion and speak evil of dignities. Sometimes believers spread stories of dreams and visions they received from the Lord about leaders. They share information that is sometimes quite damaging to the leader and ministry, which they claim to have received from the Lord.

Again, I do not want you to misunderstand me. God can and will speak to believers who are not leaders. However, if a believer's heart is not pure towards his leader and the leader has erred before God; God would not choose to show it to an individual who carries a spirit to dishonour the leader. This would be a prime opportunity to expose, disgrace and dishonour that leader.

To cover and restore that leader, God would instead reveal such information to someone who knows how to love, respect, honour, cover and restore that leader in prayer and fasting. No one with a spirit to cover would allow the devil to use them in his plan to destroy the leader, the ministry, the brother or sister. God will only reveal the weaknesses of others to those He can trust to cover them and intercede on their behalf. God is in the ministry of reconciliation and partners with those who loves the souls of others, and like Christ, wants them to be reconciled not destroyed.

Anything else is of the devil! Let me impart knowledge to you. If a believer falls from grace and goes to God in true repentance from a sincere heart; and God forgives that believer, God will never go to another believer and expose that which He has already covered under His blood; hence the reason it is so important to live holy, sanctified and righteous lives.

However, if you fall, don't stay down! Get up! Repent! Brush yourself off! Get out of the pit! Get out of the dungeon! Walk in righteousness!

The Spirit of Shem and Japheth

I admire the genius of God and His awesomeness. God never says 'Oops!' God always has a man, regardless of how wicked others choose to be. There will always be a heart that continues to honour God and a servant on whom He can rest His anointing to bring glory and honour to His name.

Shem and Japheth proved to be nothing like their brother Ham. Upon hearing the evil, embarrassing report of their father lying naked and drunk in his tent, they stopped their ears. No doubt, they screamed at Ham, rebuking him. They refused to support his show of disrespect for their father and spiritual leader. What he found amusing sparked their righteous indignation! Are there any Shem and Japheth spirits remaining within the body of Jesus Christ?

Is there anyone who is deeply wounded when a leader, brother or sister is being exposed, whether there is any truth to what is being said? I believe there are. Are you one of them? Shem and Japheth flatly refused to listen and participate in the conversation. Neither would they mock and dishonour their father.

Immediately after they learnt of their father's embarrassing situation, they took up his robe-the priestly garment- and they both laid it on their shoulders. At the entrance of the tent, they turned their backs toward the tent and entered backward so as not to view their father's nakedness.

This was a profound statement! They had no desire to discover the extent to which the story brought to them by their brother Ham was true. They never made any enquires into what might have transpired. They only needed to ensure that their father was covered! Oh my God! Their aim was to remove the reproach from their father by covering him.

They recognized something that their brother did not. Their father, even in his weakest moment, was still God's anointed vessel. They treasured the anointing on their father, Noah and were not about to allow the enemy to cause them to betray, expose or dishonour him.

Self-check! Are you a leader who covers? I told you at the beginning of this book that we are all leaders in one way or another. By design, we all have God given responsibilities beginning with having control over our own selves. We are given freewill to decide our reaction to each situation we face.

In one area of life we may serve, but even as we serve, we also lead. God gave authority to mankind at creation to

> *be fruitful, and multiply, and replenish the earth, and subdue it: and have dominion over the fish of the sea, and over the fowl of the air, and over every living thing that moveth upon the earth.*

This instruction was given to Adam. He was given the first leadership role and now needed to train the future leaders. Wherever we are placed therefore, we will either be leading or be led. Once we are in the leadership role, we are expected to cover someone. If we are being led, we are expected to honour the one who leads. I ask here again: Who are you? Are you a leader who covers or a leader who exposes?

Some persons do not enjoy these kinds of messages and might even be tempted to close their hearts as well as this book. Allowing the devil to block you from receiving this word, would only be another lost opportunity for God to minister to your spirit. He really wants to provoke you to change from the destructive path you are on and reposition yourself for a blessing.

This message is not intended to gain popularity among the masses but rather to encourage those who possess a spirit of submission to the principles of God and are holy, sanctified children of God. When I speak of sanctification, it is not referring to partial sanctification but complete surrender from the crown of your head unto the soles of your feet. Some believers are sanctified in one area while remaining filthy in others.

The anointing Noah was about to release on a son who honoured and covered him, was the same anointing coming through the generations from Adam. Adam passed it to Seth; Seth passed it to Enos; Enos passed it to Cainan before he died; Cainan bestowed it upon Mahalaleel; He passed it to Jared; Jared passed it to Enoch.

The bible tells us that Enoch walked with God and did not taste of death because he was translated to heaven. However, before he left earth, this same anointing was bestowed on Methuselah. This is the man who holds the world record in longevity; he lived for thirty one years less a millennia- a thousand years.

After carrying this anointing for nine hundred and sixty nine years, Methuselah rested it on Lamech; Lamech then placed it on Noah. Noah therefore understood how important it was for him to entrust it to someone who honours him and the source of his anointing. Noah chose Shem, one of the sons whose response to a leader in crisis was to cover and not expose!

While Japheth was also blessed, Shem received a special blessing, indicative of the anointing being transferred to him to cover the next generation and lead them on the God ordained path. Noah knew Shem could be trusted with the anointing; he passed the 'test of honour'.

Genesis 9:26

> *And he-Noah-said, Blessed be the LORD God of Shem; and Canaan shall be his servant.*
> *God shall enlarge Japheth, and he shall dwell in the tents of Shem; and Canaan shall be his servant.*

While this is not the point of emphasis here, note that although God blessed Japheth through Noah, only one leader was established here. This is another example of God's leadership principles. One leader at a time! God is not the author of confusion. I often say that anything with more than one head is a monster. God is indeed a God of order! Amen!

Can it be said of you, as it was of Shem; you have passed the 'test of honour' and is qualified to receive the anointing that rests upon your leader? Curse is passed from generation to generation in a manner similar to the passing of the anointing. Shem passed it to Arphaxad; He passed it to Salah; Salah passed it to Eber; who then passed it to Peleg. Peleg rested the same anointing coming down from Adam to Reu; He placed it on Serug and he passed it to Nahor; Nahor placed it on Terah, who bestowed it upon Abraham.

Why do you think this was chronicled in the word of God? The reason is to teach us that the anointing is transferrable! God is always looking for someone on whom He can pour out His Spirit! However, He is looking for those who -like Shem and Japheth- will cover and honour their leaders and spiritual fathers. Is that you?

This is what reveals the true nature of a leader, or aspiring leader. Every child of God should have a determination to pass the 'test of honour'. You should not want to rise against the elder but you need to respect every evangelist, missionary, chorister, deacon, usher and all other officers in the church. God admonishes believers to respect each other and obey those who are in leadership. This is shown by honouring them.

Will you?

The Spirit of Tamar

Genesis 38 shares a very interesting story of the life of one of the five women mentioned in the genealogy of Jesus. If forty two men were mentioned and only five women, I needed to take a closer look at the background of these women. What I discovered was rather interesting - they all covered the anointing!

Tamar was selected by Judah, the father of Er to marry his first son. This young man happened to be wicked in God's sight and the Lord slew him. Tamar had not borne any children prior to the death of her husband. As was the custom of Israel, Judah instructed Onan, his second son to marry Tamar and raise a seed for his deceased brother Er.

Tamar found herself in a plight. Onan's heart was also evil and he spilled his sperm on the ground, refusing to allow Tamar to conceive. He was not willing to give her a child that would be considered his deceased brother's seed. God was grieved with this behaviour and killed Onan too.

Her father-in-law Judah, came back and dictated the next move in Tamar's life. This was the obvious pattern from the beginning of the story. He instructed her to remain as a widow in her father's house until the third son, Shelah was grown. He was to be her next husband.

I am struck with admiration for her level of submission and honour for the anointing. She humbly obeyed, went back to her father's house and waited patiently. Time went by and Shelah matured to the point where he could marry Tamar. However, Judah refused to keep his end of the bargain because God had already killed two of his older sons consequent on their wickedness.

The bible lets us know that Tamar pretended to be a harlot and Judah, her father-in-law slept with her and got her pregnant. That sounds rather messy! He promised her a kid and she asked for a pledge until she received the kid. By now she had to change her strategy in dealing with Judah, since he had not proven to be a man to honour his words.

She got his signet, bracelets and staff as security and they parted company. Judah quickly sent the kid in order to get back his personal possessions. However, Tamar was nowhere to be found. She had returned to her father's house and back in her widow's garments.

This now spelt trouble for Judah, the anointed son of Israel. They tried desperately to locate the harlot but their efforts were futile. Judah was terrified that he would face embarrassment and so he called off the search and said, "Let her take it, lest we be ashamed."

Eventually, the news broke that Tamar had played the harlot and through her whoredom was pregnant. Guess what? Judah would not allow this disgrace in his family so he sent for her immediately. Her penalty was that she be burnt to death! He had no desire to ascertain with whom she had committed this abominable act. He just needed her to be punished to the full extent of the law and remove the reproach from his family.

The manner in which Tamar handled her dilemma not only landed her a place in the genealogy of Jesus but she was mentioned by name. How many women would have covered Judah like Tamar did, especially after all the times he had dealt with her unfairly? Tamar not only remained humble, submitted and obedient, she also covered the anointing.

This was a perfect opportunity to publicly disgrace Judah. Had she done that, maybe it would have been said that this is where his sons had got their wicked hearts. But Tamar knew that there was a word over Judah's life and that he was anointed to be the father of one of the twelve tribes of Israel and she covered the anointing at her own shame.

When she was brought before Judah, Tamar quietly revealed that the man whom the signet, bracelets and staff belonged to was the father of her child. Immediately, Judah's moment of indiscretion was acknowledged by him. He humbly admitted to those waiting to burn her to death and those standing by to watch her burn, "She hath been more righteous than I; because that I gave her not Shelah my son."

Tamar gave birth to twin sons, Pharez and Zarah. Although it was a messy story, God turned it into a beautiful message. Covering, instead of exposing the anointing landed her in the hall of fame as cited in Matthew chapter one.

The Spirit of Rahab

Joshua sent two spies to view the land of Jericho. They went into the house of a woman who bore the title 'Rahab the harlot.' This heathen woman immediately recognized what so many women failed to see. These men were anointed! In wisdom, even as a harlot, she did not capitalize on the opportunity to ply her trade with them. Instead she chose to cover!

The king got information that the spies had gone to Rahab's house. He subsequently sent his men with an order for her to turn them over to the authorities. However, by the time the king's men got to her house, she had already hidden the spies. She covered them from the enemy with a story so convincing, the enemy ran with it unquestioningly. Rahab attested that the men had indeed visited her house but she had no idea where they went. She even encouraged the men of Jericho to quickly pursue the spies.

Being a harlot, the king's men believed the story Rahab had fabricated and set out a wild goose chase. Whilst gone, the anointing was safely covered under the stalks of flax which Rahab had carefully laid in order upon the roof of her house. She then gave the spies classified information about Jericho's state of affairs. She told them that everyone in Jericho was fearful because they knew that the God of

Israel was God in heaven above and in earth beneath and that Jericho would be overthrown by Israel.

Rahab, like Tamar, asked for a true token that in return for her kindness would save her family. They made a deal with her; the covenant required that she placed a line of scarlet thread in her window and that all those who were connected to her, remain within her house. The men returned to the camp of Israel and reported all to Joshua.

At the conquering of Jericho, the promise made to Rahab - 'the harlot' was kept and she along with her family members, were engrafted into the family of God. Like Tamar, that which Rahab had done was remarkable. She too made it to the hall of fame in the genealogy of Jesus recorded in Matthew 1:5,

And Salmon begat Booz of Rachab.

I was very deliberate in making mention of her in the same manner that the book of Joshua did because it reminds me of the actions of some believers within the body of Christ today. In the book of Joshua, she was constantly referred to as 'Rahab the harlot'. Even when our past is under the blood, many believers continue to dwell on who we were as an act of dishonouring the anointing which God has placed on our lives. Don't lose confidence! Instead, declare boldly that your present position and your past is by no means an indication of your future potential in God!

Here, Rahab covered the anointing and was blessed by God. Her name continues to ring out today among believers as a virtuous woman. Are there any Rahabs reading? Continue to cover and honour the anointing, God will give you a place in the kingdom that will blow the minds of your haters and they will be able to do nothing about it! Hallelujah!

The Spirit of Ruth

Some believers should be blessed a long time ago! But they dishonoured the anointing and their blessings have been delayed. God is waiting until they know how to honour the anointing that releases huge breakthroughs.

The Lord told me that some are covetous, every time they see someone walk towards me and plant a seed (money) at my feet. However, God says that whatever one sows into the anointing that they will also reap. If you feel like sowing into the anointing, go ahead and do as you are led. God honours your faith and your seed. Your harvest is guaranteed because God is faithful and true. He cannot lie!

The bible also tells of a woman by the name of Naomi who had two daughters in law, Ruth and Orpah. After the death of her husband and two sons, she decided to go back to Bethlehem, her native land. Orpah eventually told her she could go ahead without her. She turned from following Naomi and went back to her kinfolks in Moab. Ruth acted otherwise! She was able to recognize the anointing on her mother-in-law and told her this:

> *Intreat me not to leave thee, or to return from following after thee: for whither thou goest, I will go; and where thou lodgest, I will lodge: thy people shall be my people, and thy God my God:*
> *Where thou diest, will I die, and there will I be buried: the LORD do so to me, and more also, if ought but death part thee and me.* Ruth 1:16-17

Can you make that kind of commitment to your leader if you recognize the anointing on his life and ministry? "Go ahead my bishop I am not leaving the church; your people will be my people; your God shall be my God." Will you rest in the anointing and declare: "I am not running from the church. When we go through the fire, I am staying with the ministry. When we go through the water, I am staying with the ministry."

There is a reward for those who honour the anointing. Ruth took the decision to stay with Naomi and to suffer with her. She said, "I know that you do not have a son to give me to marry but I am still not leaving you."

Naomi went back to Beth-le-hem, which is translated, House of Bread. Naomi decided to return to the 'House of Bread' with confidence in her God's goodness. She thought to herself, "My God is good. He will feed me."

While Ruth was with her, daily she went to the field of Boaz and began to glean. Initially, the gleaning was only a 'hand to mouth' provision. But! But! But! God was actually setting her up. You will recall that she was not a Jew but a Moabitess, a Gentile. Nonetheless, she tapped into the anointing.

Tap into the anointing! Do not dishonour it! Tap into it! Tap into it! Tap into it! How can you tap into the anointing? I believe that you have got the revelation by now. Honour it! You tap into the anointing, by honouring it.

I was told of a young man who heard his employer and coworkers, speaking ill of his pastor. He not only expressed his disapproval of what they were doing but demanded that they discontinued their blatant disregard for his leader. They did not desist and he walked off the job.

Now that is honour - the kind which is appreciated by the pastor and on which God also smiles. I have witnessed God's provision for that young man. He was given a beautiful wife as well as a lush wedding at absolutely no cost to him at all, at all, at all! God gave him a better job too. Guess what? God took care of him because he honoured his pastor's anointing. No need to be covetous - honour the anointing, as he wisely did and God will bless you also.

Ruth sat at Naomi's feet. She was not to marry a Jew because God said that the Jews should not mix with the Gentiles. But she remained under Naomi's anointing, giving honour to it. She would not go anywhere without Naomi's approval, even in the face of hunger and thirst. If it were now, she might have sung, "I am waiting down here by the river till you come Lord Jesus."

The bible says that because she honoured the anointing, she attracted the attention of Boaz. As a preacher, God spoke to me about my personal life. In response, I have decided that I will never marry a woman who dishonours the anointing of God on my life. Ruth sat there under the anointing of Naomi and not only listened to her instructions but obeyed them.

Naomi cautioned her to avoid any display of inappropriate behaviour. She was to go out with the maidens of Boaz only. In doing so, she would never be seen in anyone else's field. She obeyed and sure enough Boaz noticed that a stranger was among his servants. He enquired of them who she was.

He was informed that she was Naomi's daughter-in-law and that her husband had died. Boaz' heart was moved by the Lord, this resulted in Ruth receiving double anointing. He subsequently instructed his servants to leave a double portion behind as they harvested the grain.

The bible says that Boaz fell in love with Ruth and married her. Here again, like Moses, another Jew had stepped out of line, regarding the instruction which God gave and married another Gentile woman. Boaz, how could you have done that?

God saw that Ruth carried the heart of a Jew, honouring the anointing on Naomi. So while the children of Israel were dishonouring the anointing, God saw a Gentile who identified the anointing and honoured it.

God rewarded her by adopting her into the family of Israel when she married Boaz. Boaz, as you will recall, was not an ordinary Jew. He came from the line of Judah. Note too that like Ruth, Tamar and Rahab named in the genealogy of Jesus were Gentiles.

Booz begat Obed of RUTH; and Obed begat Jesse;

And Jesse begat David the king; and David the king begat Solomon of her that had been the wife of Urias;

And Solomon begat Roboam; and Roboam begat Abia; and Abia begat Asa;

And Asa begat Josaphat; and Josaphat begat Joram; and Joram begat Ozias;

And Ozias begat Joatham; and Joatham begat Achaz; and Achaz begat Ezekias;

And Ezekias begat Manasses; and Manasses begat Amon; and Amon begat Josias;

And Josias begat Jechonias and his brethren, about the time they were carried away to Babylon:

And after they were brought to Babylon. Jechonias begat Salathiel; and Salathiel begat Zorobabel;

And Zorobabel begat Abiud; and Abiud begat Eliakin; and Eliakim begat Azor;

And Azor begat Sadoc; and Sadoc begat Achim; and Achim begat Eliud;

And Eliud begat Eleazar; and Eleazar begat Matthan; and Matthan begat Jacob; And Jacob begat Joseph the husband of Mary, of whom was born JESUS, who is called CHRIST. Matthew 1

One woman who was humble and honoured the anointing, entered the hall of fame in the Royal family and her name is one of the only four women named in the genealogy of Jesus. There is an extraordinary blessing for the women who choose to cover and not expose the anointing.

This is a great self-check point for women in the body of Christ. What is your resolve? Can you truly say from a sincere heart that you will honour the men who God has anointed and placed in your lives? This is important at home, work, church and in other spheres of life.

The Spirit of David

The prophet Samuel in 1 Samuel 16:1-13 was sent by God to the house of Jesse with a view to anointing one of his sons as king of Israel. There, all seven sons in Jesse's house passed before him and God chose none.

Eventually, David was presented to him and according to verses 12 and 13 which state:

> *And he sent, and brought him in. Now he was ruddy, and withal of a beautiful countenance, and the LORD said, "Arise, anoint him for this is he.*
>
> *Then Samuel took the horn of oil and anointed him in the midst of his brethren: and the Spirit of the Lord came upon David from that day forward."*

Samuel poured the horn of oil on David and told him that he was anointed; he had been chosen by God to be the next king of Israel.

Meanwhile, the Spirit of the Lord departed from Saul who was at that time reigning as king of Israel. Consequently, Saul rose against David with one resolve - to kill him. David began running and hiding.

One day, he ended up in a cave and while there, Saul entered the cave also. David went over to him, took out his sword and cut a piece of his skirt privately. Eventually, Saul rose and got out of the cave; David followed suit and cried after Saul. When Saul turned around, he saw David stooping with his face to the earth, bowing himself before King Saul.

> *Then David said, "Wherefore hearest thou men's words, saying, Behold, David seeketh thy hurt?*

Behold, this day thine eyes have seen how that the LORD had delivered thee today into mine hand in the cave: and some bade me kill thee: but mine eye spared thee; and I said, I will not put forth mine hand against my lord; for he is the LORD's anointed.

Moreover, my father, see, yea, see the skirt of the robe in my hand: for in that I cut off the skirt of thy robe, and killed thee not, know thou that there is neither evil nor transgression in mine hand." 1 Samuel 24:9-11

In today's discourse and Jamaican parlance, David would have probably said, "Oh Daddy Saul, mi know yuh desparately trying fi kill me! But! But! But! Me nuh stay like yuh, caus last night mi get a chance fi dun yuh; but me nah touch di Lawd's anointed". In other words – Saul, I practiced what I learnt about the anointing."

Saul may have responded in this manner, "So why didn't you take it and kill me?" To which David may have responded, "How could I touch the Lord's anointed? Saul, I know who you are! The prophet Samuel had called you out; poured a vial of oil on your head and anointed you to be captain over His inheritance. That makes you an anointed vessel of God. As long as the anointing was placed on you, I refuse to touch you."

David decided not to touch Saul but rather to leave him to the Lord. I can just imagine in the realm of the spirit that after David had done that, God looked down on him, smiled and called over Gabriel and said to him, "Hey Gabriel, David just passed the 'test of honour'! He got the perfect opportunity to slay Saul but covered him instead." He had an awareness of his responsibility to cover the anointing and it propelled him to make the wise decision to let him be.

Hear me today! If David had killed Saul, there would never have been a King David. Don't do it! If you love yourself, don't dare to do it! If you love God, don't do it! If you want God to use you, don't touch your leader! Touch not the Lord's anointed! Leave him alone!

David was running from Saul when he went into the cave. The men who surrounded David were renowned men of war who at one point in their lives were heavily indebted and stressed. They all ran to David in the cave, where he ministered to them and became a captain over them. Having encouraged them, he then brought them out of the cave.

At the prophet's command, David emerged from the cave of Adullam with them and went to Judah. Those men remained loyal to David. They never left him because they realized that David was God's anointed. They had both seen and experienced the manifested glory of God on David's life. They watched as God used the little shepherd boy to slay the mighty Goliath with only a sling and a stone. They had also witnessed the hand of God on David's life, as He transformed him into a phenomenal sword fighter. David himself testified that God taught his hands to war. Initially, he neither possessed the knowledge nor the skills in wielding the sword.

The men were with David when he fell into adultery with Bathsheba. They were there with him when he committed murder to get rid of Bathsheba's husband, Uriah. They remained steadfast in their loyalty, commitment and honour toward David when his "back was against the wall." They covered the anointed servant of God just the same! They backed him up with prayer and fasting, while guarding the anointing. They were with him until the kingdom was restored unto David. They were with him to the end of his days on earth.

Their names are recorded in the Hall of Fame in 2 Samuel 23, where David celebrated all thirty seven of them. God acknowledged their honour for the anointing, during the forty years which they were with David.

Should the Lord tarry for another forty years, who would still be honouring the anointing and those whom God used in their life? Who would still be in the church defending the anointing? When the building expands to five times its present size and the ministry has over fifty locations, who will still be covering the anointing?

APOSTLE WINSTON G. BAKER

Who will be able to say, "I was there when the bishop was down? I was there when the bishop was up? I never ran away whenever the ministry was under attack. I remained faithful and committed even when it was under pressure. I stood with the ministry, covered it with my prayer, fasting and support."

There is no ministry that God establishes which does not go through fire. As long as God ordains a ministry, there will be both mountain top and valley experiences. There will be seasons of rejoicing but also times of war.

I am able to readily identify the hypocrites in church. Their spirits are so open in the presence of the anointing that it makes it difficult for them to hide who they really are. There would be those who come to declare their love for me, with hugs and kisses which could leave my jaws raw. They boast of how much they pray and fast for me, yet in their hearts they desire to see my demise.

None of this impresses me! Their flattery does not move me. Like David, I know real committed, dedicated and honouring men. As a boy coming from the streets, having experience in the sports and entertainment industries, I know real fans.

Michael Jackson had some real fans! They curled their hair like him. They bleached their skin and wore pants, shoes, gloves and belt like him. They perfect the moon walk -his popular dance move- and knew all the music from his sound tracks. They were his fans!

Closer home to Jamaicans is the most recent dancehall sensation which has led to tattooing, bleaching, a particular brand shoes and a specific way of dress. The die-hearted fans of this entertainer remain loyal whether he is free or incarcerated. No one is permitted to speak evil of him without offending his fans.

David was a real warrior and a real God fan! He stated unapologetically that he hated those who hate his God. His position was quite clear: "If you hate my God, don't come around me." There goes a real God fan!

88

So too is it for me: If you hate my God, you can't be my friend. An atheist cannot be my friend! How can you say that you are my friend, when your best friend is an enemy of mine who speaks all manner of evil against me? I told you before that I cannot be fooled. Like the eagle, I test before I trust!

Hear what David had to say in Psalm 139:19-22:

> *Surely thou wilt slay the wicked, O God: depart from me therefore, ye bloody men.*
>
> *For they speak against Thee wickedly, and Thine enemies take Thy name in vain.*
>
> *Do not I hate them, O LORD, that hate Thee? And am not I grieved with those that rise up against Thee?*
>
> *I hate them with perfect hatred: I count them mine enemies.*

This is a good time for a self-check! Give God praise, if you have not touched God's anointed.

The Spirit of Elisha

The spirit of Elisha is characterized by humility and total commitment to servant-hood without any desire to usurp authority. It is a spirit which holds leaders in high regard while not giving them the glory and honour that belongs to God. The spirit of Elisha is able to recognize the anointing of God on a leader and acknowledges that in honouring the leader, he is honouring the one who has anointed the leader.

The spirit of Elisha displays a similar commitment to leadership as Ruth. It is willing to follow even in the face of impending danger, death or any other form of separation. The high level of respect and honour given to leadership by one who carries the spirit of Elisha is expressed in the very language used in addressing the leader.

In 1 Kings 19:16, God instructed Elijah to anoint Elisha to be prophet in his room. Elijah obeyed the Lord's command when he threw his mantle on him. This was done while he passed by Elisha plowing with the oxen. Noteworthy, is the fact that Elisha left the oxen and followed Elijah from that day in the servant position. The bible says that

he arose and went after Elijah, and ministered unto him.

Throughout the scriptures, there was no mention of Elisha's name as Elijah continued his prophetic ministry. Instead, there were a few references made of Elijah's servant. He was so inconspicuous that after Elijah's translation, he was embarrassingly referred to as 'Elisha the son of Shaphat, which poured water on the hand of Elijah'. This was how one of the king's servants saw him even though he occupied the office of an anointed prophet. They did not acknowledge his prophetic anointing. However, he knew both his calling and his anointing and was therefore not concerned with pleasing men but with pleasing God.

At the point which God was ready to transfer the anointing from Elijah to Elisha, he had to do the 'test of honour'. Elisha's 'stick-to-it-iveness' was being used to measure his honour and commitment to serving Elijah to the end. This decision made him a mockery in Israel.

He first encountered the sons of the prophets at Bethel. They came to him saying,

"Knowest thou that the LORD will take away thy master from thy head today?"

He responded in the affirmative but advised them to hold their peace! Their efforts to dissuade Elisha from following his leader to the end were futile.

Elijah himself tried to persuade Elisha to stay in Bethel because the Lord had sent him to Jericho. By now Elisha was cognizant that to honour the anointing required that he remained in close connection to the anointed one. Respectfully, Elisha told Elijah that he was determined to cleave to this anointing and wherever he went, he would follow.

Can the spirit of Elisha be identified readily in emerging leaders within the body of Christ? Is there any who realizes that God's hands are on you to do a mighty work in these end times but He has placed you under leadership? God sometimes places us under authority to develop character in us. We must be humble enough to minister to the needs of our leaders, while God prepares us for promotion. Are you the kind of emerging leader who continues to cover and honour your leader, even when others speak evil of him and make a mockery of your loyalty? Can you boldly declare in the face of ridicule that I am not moving from under the anointing that God used to deliver me?

The Lord gave me a word for those with a disloyal and dishonouring spirit. As a leader, he said to me, "All those who have determined in their hearts to enter into rebellion, let them go!" The Lord told me that if they want to leave the church, I should not be afraid to let them leave.

However, He said that I should let them know that the demons which the enemy has assigned to destroy them are anxiously waiting. They want believers to remove themselves from under the anointing which covers them and detach themselves from the church through rebellion. As soon as the devil steals them from under the anointing which covered them, the door will be opened for the demons to wreak havoc in their lives. No one will be able to minister deliverance to them as long as their lives are characterized by rebellion and dishonour.

We must bear in mind, that although there are several physical structures in which people gather for worship; that is not the church! The true church is the body of our Lord and Saviour, Jesus Christ. It is not divided by geographical boundaries. Divisions within the body of Christ are only possible through disobedience to the principles and commands outlined within the word of God. This equates to disobedience to the Spirit of God.

What believers sometimes forget is that God looks at the heart of each individual. Much of what is manifesting when persons leave a congregation with a fault-finding spirit, is really a public demonstration of the spirit of rebellion which has gone unchecked for a long time. Like Ham, the life of that believer attracts curses!

The question is: What are you going to do when you leave yourself uncovered and the enemy comes in like a flood to steal, kill and destroy you? Where will you run to? My God! The Spirit of the Lord exposed the acts of some members who want to leave the ministry. As part of their strategy to form an alliance with another place of worship, they begin to withhold their tithes from where God placed them. They then begin to sow it into another ministry which they eventually hope to become a part of.

God considers those actions equivalent to that of the foolish virgins. These behaviours are characteristic of believers who are lacking in wisdom and knowledge of God. They are ignorant of the principles of God concerning leadership and do not really understand who God is.

In summary, God knows hearts and judges actions based on motives. A leader who is sure that God has chosen him; anointed him and appointed him to serve in any ministry, need not fear any of these spirits. For wherever God guides, He provides and whenever God gives a vision, He makes the provision. A leader sent by God is never alone! While he leads, he confidently follows God's leading! This formula guarantees success in any given situation!

Elisha knew all too well that purity is all that can come in God's presence and that eliminated any reservations he had of continuing with Elijah to the end. He knew that in honouring Elijah and ministering to him, he was honouring God. He was also cognizant that there was blessing in obedience. It is clear that Elisha intended to get something in return for his faithfulness.

Elisha had to go through four stages: Gilgal to Bethel; Bethel to Jericho; Jericho to Jordan and from Jordan to the chariot of fire. On completing the third stage of the journey, as they crossed the river Jordan, Elijah asked Elisha what he wanted him to do for him before he was taken away. Elisha requested that a double portion of his spirit rest upon him. Elijah then said to him:

If thou see me when I am taken up from thee, it shall be
so unto thee; but if not, it shall not be so.

There came a whirlwind; a tornado. It was not just powerful winds rotating violently but this funnel shaped system swooped everything in its path. It is usually dark too! It must have been rather challenging for Elisha's focus to remain on Elijah in the midst of this destructive vortex of air. Nonetheless, Elisha refused to take his eyes off the anointed one! To pass this test guaranteed him a double portion of that which was on his master, Elijah. He was not about to miss this 'once in a lifetime opportunity!'

You have to learn to hold on, if you need a double portion of the anointing that rests on your leader. You must remain focused! There is a tornado; a whirlwind sweeping through the body of Christ. Missiles and debris are flying all around. It is aimed at distracting believers from receiving the benefits of the anointing. Believers who lose their focus will be caught up in the isms and schisms that weaken their faith and effectiveness in the kingdom of God.

A wise believer will take cover from the flying missiles and remain focused on the anointing. Focused believers are always eager to see the glory of God being manifested through an anointed vessel. They are aware of the fact that the ability to identify and connect with an anointed vessel, is to be perfectly positioned as a recipient of a double portion on that which is on him.

The same robe Adam lost; the same robe for which Cain murdered Abel; the same robe Lamech handed to Noah; the same robe which

Noah gave to Shem who became the Melchizedek, the priest of Salem and king of Jerusalem; the same robe that Joseph received from Jacob; the same robe which was upon Elijah; this same robe was now about to be released into another generation.

The 'test of honour' was given to Elisha, who passed even in the midst of a whirlwind! Elijah was caught up in the chariot of fire and that which Elisha yearned for fell from Elijah. It was now Elisha's turn to wear that robe. He bent down and took it up!

Chapter Five

Strange Warfare

The whole concept of Christianity is warfare!

However, it is rather comforting as a leader in the body of Christ to have the assurance that the blood of Jesus covers me. I have found it necessary to constantly make this declaration over my life: The blood of Jesus covers me! It is good to proclaim it wherever we go. Let those we come in contact with know that we are covered by the blood of Jesus.

Leaders within the body of Christ should place that coverage not only over their lives and affairs but also over the lives of those whom they lead. Of equal importance is the need to teach members of our household and congregation to also make this declaration over their lives and their family respectively.

The body of Christ is under attack! Leaders are the prime targets. The devil knows pretty well that if he smites the shepherd, the sheep of the flock shall be scattered abroad, Matthew 26:31. You are engaged in a strange warfare. There are many unexpected battles facing leaders within the body of Christ today, but God says to tell you, "Do not worry - you are covered."

That assurance is reason to celebrate! Shout for joy and rejoice in the fact that victory is ours! David detailed in Psalm 121 a number of ways in which the Lord covers His people. He says:

> *I will lift up mine eyes unto the hills, from whence cometh my help.*
>
> *My help cometh from the LORD, which made heaven and earth.*
>
> *He will not suffer thy foot to be moved: He that keepeth thee will not slumber.*
>
> *Behold, He that keepeth Israel shall neither slumber nor sleep.*
>
> *The LORD is thy keeper: the LORD is thy shade upon thy right hand.*
>
> *The sun shall not smite thee by day, nor the moon by night.*
>
> *The LORD shall preserve thee from all evil: He shall preserve thy soul.*
>
> *The LORD shall preserve thy going out and thy coming in from this time forth, and even for evermore.*

David was a warrior, engaging in battles from his youthful days. Biblical records inform us that his first two battles were not with men but with ravenous beasts. It is well known that he was placed behind his father's house to care for sheep as a young boy. This gave birth to David's first career as a shepherd boy.

While executing his duties as caretaker for his father's sheep, David reported that on different occasions beasts came and took lambs from the flock. In each instance, he chased the beast, smote it and delivered the sheep from its mouth. The beasts then rose against David himself. He caught, smote and killed them both. The anointing which God had placed on David was manifesting as he defeated the beasts.

Naturally, David began acquiring knowledge in the nature and characteristics of sheep. Undoubtedly, he discovered their helplessness and knew he was their only defense against their enemies. Imagine, if you will, how those poor sheep cried as they were being snatched away by the mean lion and ferocious bear. David's response to grab his staff and advance towards the direction of the sheep's cry was more than likely, instinctive. The scene of the helpless lambs clutched within their powerful jaws must have been frightening. That protective nature of David the shepherd boy had to be what triggered his spontaneous reaction.

Without hesitation or contemplation, David attacked them, freed his sheep and eventually killed them. What took place can only be described by one word-SUPERNATURAL!

Whenever God calls and appoints a leader, He also anoints them. That which David felt was the anointing. It moved through his entire being, releasing adrenaline and supernaturally empowering him with the boldness and strength to rip the sheep from the clutches of the beasts.

In the process, David discovered something about himself which he did not know before. He had power! It took an incident to unearth the anointing! There David, as a little boy, experienced the glory. This is a prime example of how God operates with the anointing. There is seemingly, always a secret place; a quiet time; a remote state; a behind the scene where He hides the emerging leader. There He trains and tests them before showcasing the anointing on centre stage.

Preceding any grand display of the glory of God in a leader's life, there is always a time of preparation. This usually takes place in confinement as He trains His warriors in privacy. David, in appearance was only a boy. His locale made him inconspicuous. Nonetheless, his relationship with God was being developed from level to level.

Right there in obscurity, he developed the proclivity to pen his thoughts, experiences, prayers and petitions which he made to God. He wrote numerous songs, many of which have become well known in

Christendom. Although he wrote from a place of isolation and rejection, he was not alone. His writings revealed that in those dark moments God manifested presence was astoundingly evident.

I find it rather challenging to write or speak about David without mentioning the fact that he was the 'black sheep' of his family. Bible scholars have postulated that he was born out of wedlock and had the ascribed status of a bastard. Consequently, he was rejected by the other members of David's lawful household.

Like many rejected persons, David resorted to journaling. In Psalm 27:10, he pens these words:

> When my father and my mother forsake me, then the LORD will take me up.

He continued to express his emotional hurt in Psalm 34:6 in saying:

> This poor man cried, and the LORD heard him, and saved him out of all his troubles.

Note that in both instances, His comfort and confidence rested in God's intervention and deliverance.

David was behind the scenes but God was obviously with him. In the fullness of time, God decided that David's moment to be repositioned from the back to the front had arrived. As part of the process in accomplishing this plan, God divinely orchestrated **a situation in order to give a revelation.**

This is characteristic of God, to create **a situation in order to bring about a revelation!** Repeatedly, He allows some things to happen which results in the discovery or revelation of an ability or gift that not even the individual knew he possessed. It was hidden not just from onlookers but from the individual himself.

In David's case, God allowed a champion warrior to arise from within the camp of the Philistines, which no one from the Israelites camp dared to challenge. No one possessed the faith or confidence to face the mighty giant, Goliath of Gath.

This is an opportune time to remind leaders within the body of Christ that the hotter the battle, the sweeter shall be the victory! The more intense the warfare, the greater will be your anointing to secure victory. As a boy, my father and grandmother always repeated this Jamaican proverb in my hearing, "If di fowl a guh big, it show from di foot." In other words there are observable traits in the early stages of one's development, which gives an indication of their future potential for greatness.

Similarly, a leader who God calls can have a fair idea of the magnitude of the ministry which God has given to him, by observing the intensity of the fire, opposition, challenges and attacks he faces. Even with new believers, a key factor in determining the level of anointing that will be poured into their lives is to observe the level of warfare they encounter on entering the ministry.

God allowed Israel to desire a king; then created an opportunity to reposition David from behind his father's house to the throne and palace. Goliath shouted, "Bring me a warrior!" King Saul was the chief of Israel during this crisis and should be the one to respond to Goliath's challenge. However, Saul and all Israel were very fearful and dismayed.

In the interim, Jesse called his son David and instructed him to go to Bethlehem with parched corn and bread for his brothers and cheese for their captain of thousand. I know you are quite familiar with the story and remember well how on reaching Bethlehem, David heard the uproar. In response to his enquiry as to the reason for the noise, he was informed of Goliath's challenge to Israel.

David's astounding response came in the form of a question, "Who is this uncircumcised Philistine, that he should defy the armies of the living God?" He immediately volunteered to challenge Goliath. Prior to giving his consent, he had asked how the person who defeated this giant would be rewarded. He was told that the person would become the king's son in law and his father's house being exempted from paying taxes.

As attractive as these sounded to David, it was his anger at Goliath's disdain for the God of Israel that fuelled his desire to destroy him. The reward was secondary. David wondered how he could be so bold to rise against God's people. He said to them, "Send me over there, I will go and fight him." In today's jargon, "Let me go deal with his case. I will fix him!"

God again worked through David in a supernatural way! This time, with only one stone, he defeated the mighty Philistine champion - Goliath of Gath. Israel now had the enemy on the move; they began to run for their lives. The Israelites drew their swords and ravished them.

King Saul ordered that the little boy David be brought to him for an interview. Immediately following, David was promoted to being a captain in the army of God. At Saul's request David again entered into the enemy's camp and again God empowered him. This time he destroyed two hundred Philistines and brought back their foreskins to King Saul.

A secret lies in David's return to Israel swinging the reproductive organs of two hundred men in the air. This act was a public declaration to the enemy that I have destroyed your seed; I am stopping an increase in your generation. This was a proclamation of championship! On every entry into the enemy's camp, David had emerged victorious.

Over time, David had fought and won many battles. He sat and reflected on the victories God had given him. God had taken David from behind his father's house and made him captain of the greatest army on the earth. He is the one now leading the army of God into battle. This was a fulfillment of the secret prophecy over his life by the prophet Samuel that he would be the king of Israel but it was not yet known to Saul. David took up his pen and began to write again; this time he wrote the popular Psalm 27:

The LORD is my light and my salvation; whom shall I fear? The LORD is the strength of my life; of whom shall I be afraid?

When the wicked, even mine enemies and my foes, came upon me to eat up my flesh, they stumbled and fell.

Let us pause here to closely examine these two verses. David could not be referring to human beings here, as it is not natural for human beings to eat the flesh of other humans. Obviously this was written as David reflected on his experience with the lion and the bear which was mentioned earlier. Notice how he penned the outcome, **"they stumbled and fell."**

This should serve as an encouragement for us that the same God who met your financial obligations the last time; the same God who opened doors for the children last year, will without fail do it again! Go ahead and encourage yourself with the words of the song:

He'll do it again for you; He'll do it again
Just take a look at where you are now and where you have been
Hasn't He always come through for you, He's the same now as then
You may not know how, you may not know when
But He'll do it again.

David began walking with God and was established by Him. Finally, he sat on the throne having amassed a wealth of experience. Being a veteran warrior, he is now surrounded by a contingent of mighty warriors; violent men of war. It was virtually impossible for anyone to get by these men whom God had placed around him. In order to enter the presence of the king, these mighty warriors had to grant permission. Yet, this was not where David's confidence lay when he declared that, "I am covered!" His coverage came from the Lord. As believers and leaders in the body of Christ, we too can boldly declare, "We are covered!"

To exegete Psalm 121, you will agree with other bible scholars that David did not write here as a shepherd boy. Neither was this Psalm written soon after he ascended to the throne but rather when he was an old man. It was written long after he was still able to swing the sword as skilfully as he did in his youthful exuberance.

So David wrote this Psalm when he was old and stricken in years. He was no longer humanly capable of slaying a hundred Philistines. Yet he was engaged in warfare at this point in his life. The battle he fought at this juncture was a strange one and quite similar to that in which we are currently engaged as leaders.

The bible recorded for our benefit, how David responded to this strange battle. He said

> *"I will lift up mine eyes unto the hills from whence cometh my help."*

This impresses upon us the fact that this strange warfare does not warrant the use of the sword as previous ones did. Neither could he depend on the expertise of the mighty warriors who stood securely by him.

The Philistine's camp was not where this new battle emerged. As a matter of fact, it was not coming from the outside at all, at all, at all! This was unlike that which he faced with Saul; it was an inside job! Unfortunately, the enemy he faced was one from his own loins, Absalom his son.

Absalom was so absorbed with passion to become the king of Israel that he was willing to kill his own father to get there. Driven by his ego, he resorted to doing anything that he believed would result in a premature end to David's reign and place him as leader over Israel. Earlier, we exposed the spirit of Absalom, but now we will reveal the nature and characteristics of the leader who covered, even as Absalom dishonoured.

Now, David, the leader is under attack and he cannot respond with a sword because his heart is knitted with the one who has risen up against him. The pureness of his heart towards Absalom and the depth of his love for the son of his loins, restrained him from taking any defensive action.

Likewise, whenever the spirit of Absalom raises its ugly head within the body of Christ, the anointed leader, will not want to see any hurt come to the one who the enemy is using. He will endeavour to avoid any kind of confrontation and resist any desire to see the person backslide. Instead, the leader who covers begins to seek for a way to escape, wanting to save the child whom he has begotten in Christ Jesus.

David had to run! He left his house to the keeping of some concubines and went into hiding because of someone who was utilizing David's influence on his life to overthrow him. There would never be an Absalom without a David. It was David whom God had called and not Absalom. In order to avoid a confrontation, David was very careful to hide the evil report he received from Absalom. It must have been painful for the king to hear that there was a conspiracy against his life. But to learn that his own son, whom he loved, was the instigator must have been unbearable!

Indeed a strange battle! Leaders today facing similar attacks must be careful to seek God's direction and avoid fleshly responses to these painful and potentially destructive situations. There are times when God is saying, "This battle is a strange battle; the enemy is a member of your own household. The enemy is one for whom you have fasted and prayed. The enemy is one whom you have covered. Let me handle it!"

Sometimes you will discover that the offender is the child-natural or spiritual-whom you treasure most. While David was on the run, he met Shimei who began to stone and curse him. Notice too that whenever a leader comes under attack from within, enemies from the outside seize the opportunity to attack as well.

Shimei's hatred for David was ongoing for years but never surfaced until the warfare with his own son became public knowledge. As soon as someone in the church or home rises against his leaders, those on the outside are empowered to attack and disrespect those leaders too.

And when King David came to Bahurim, behold, thence came out a man of the family of the house of Saul, whose name was Shimei, the son of Gera: he came forth, and cursed still as he came.

And he cast stones at David, and at all the servants of King David: and all the people and all the mighty men were on his right hand and on his left.

And thus said Shimei when he cursed, Come out, come out, thou bloody man of Belial:

The LORD hath returned upon thee all the blood of the house of Saul, in whose stead thou hast reigned; and the Lord hath delivered the kingdom into the hand of Absalom thy son: and, behold thou art taken in thy mischief, because thou art a blood man.

Then said Abishai the son of Zeruiah unto the king, Why should this dead dog curse my lord the king? Let me go over, I pray thee, and take off his head.

And the king said, What have I to do with you, ye sons of Zeruiah? So let him curse, because the LORD hath said unto him, Curse David. Who shall then say, Wherefore hast thou done so?

And David said to Abishai, and to all his servants, Behold, my son, which came forth of my bowels, seeketh my life: how much more now may this Benjamite do it? Let him alone, and let him curse; for the LORD hath bidden him.

It may be that the LORD will look on mine affliction, and that the LORD will requite me good for his cursing this day.

And as David and his men went by the way, Shimei went along on the hill's side over against him, and cursed as he went, and threw stones at him, and cast dust. 2 Samuel 16:5-13

There will come a time in your life when those you love will rise against you too. Persons for whom you have fasted, prayed and interceded will conspire against you. Even those whom you have fed and helped in their times of need and crises, will become your enemy. Observe David's response in this situation and be wise enough to practice that which you learnt whenever you are faced with a similar situation.

I told you that this is a strange warfare! But these battles also arise in strange places. If God calls and anoints you to lead, there will be times in your life when choir members will rise against you. Do not be alarmed if even the choir director can't tolerate you anymore. Right there on the ministerial board, missionary board, usher board, deacon board and among evangelists, strange battles arise. Someone does not want to see you occupy the office which God has given you.

What are you going to do? Just relax and say, "My God will see me through this one. I am going to trust Him to keep me. I will not fight for myself; God will fight for me."

Shimei hurled condemnatory insults at David, there are people within the body of Christ who will point fingers at you in your moments of difficulty. They conclude that you are under attack as a result of something wrong which you have done. Shimei was just as wrong as they usually are.

You know the truth that David had not taken the throne from Saul. Disobedience is what caused him to lose the throne. His was the decision to please people instead of God. God commanded Saul to go and smite Amalek, and utterly destroy all that they had. He was told not to spare them but to slay both man and woman, infant and suckling, ox and sheep, camel and ass. Utterly destroy!

Saul went in and began to slay until he got to Agag, the king. He, along with his people saved the king, as well as the best of the sheep, oxen, fatlings, lambs and all that were good. Saul pleased the people, disregarding God's command. The excuse was that these were being reserved to be used as sacrifice. However, God was interested in obedience above sacrifice.

Consequently, God sent Samuel the priest, to inform Saul that the kingdom would be taken from him because of his disobedience. When Samuel arrived, Saul said to him,

> *"Blessed be thou of the LORD: I have performed the commandment of the LORD.* Samuel asked him *"What meaneth then this bleating of the sheep in mine ears, and the lowing of the oxen which I hear?"*

Saul said,

> *"They have brought them from the Amalekites: for the people spared the best of the sheep and of the oxen, to sacrifice unto the LORD thy God; and the rest we have utterly destroyed."*

Samuel told him that God had rejected him as king and has given the throne to his neighbour because he is better than him. So Shimei had it all wrong when he cursed David; he totally misrepresented the facts.

David did not take the kingdom, Saul lost it! David was only anointed! Can you relate? Then declare: I am anointed! I am anointed! I am hated because I am anointed! They fight against me because I am anointed! I am surrounded by enemies because I am anointed!

When you are anointed, you don't need to do anything to anyone for them to rise against you. If you dress well, they will fight against you; if you dress poorly, they will still rise against you. So what are you going to do? Clearly it is not you, it is the anointing!

You will recall that the spirit of Absalom is the spirit that wants to be you. It wants to get you out of the way so that it can be you. It wants to imitate you, but to get the opportunity; it must first get rid of you. It is important that leaders who experience these strange attacks remember that God is the One who called you. God is the One who anointed you. Let those with the Absalom spirit know, "I did not ask for this anointing; I did not choose myself for leadership." Let them know that from you were in your mother's womb God predestined you; God anointed you; God called you.

Whenever God calls you, no witchcraft can kill you. They can burn all the candles they want; do all the voodoo, 'hoodoo', black magic, white magic and any other evils they wish. If God calls you, no sorcery can touch you! Tell the devil, "Hands off!"

The God, who calls me, will fight for me. I need neither gun nor knife; neither do I need to use my fist. I have a weapon nonetheless! I know what to do when these strange attacks come upon me. I just get on my knees like David and say,

> *"Hear my cry, O God; attend unto my prayer. From the end of the earth will I cry unto thee, when my heart is overwhelmed: lead me to the rock that is higher than I.* Psalm 61:1-2

This warfare is a strange warfare; so what are you going to do? I will lift up mine eyes unto the hills from whence cometh my help, all my help cometh from the Lord. My help is here! God told me to tell you that your help is here! Your deliverance is here! He says that weeping may endure for a night but joy cometh in the morning. Your joy is here! Your joy is here!

There is assurance in the word of God:

> *They that wait upon the LORD shall renew their strength; they shall mount up with wings as eagles; they shall*

APOSTLE WINSTON G. BAKER

run, and not be weary; and they shall walk, and not faint.
Isaiah 40:31

He that keeps you never slumbers or sleeps. Our God does not wear pajamas; our God does not go to bed. God wants us to be at peace even in the midst of these strange attacks. Because He does not sleep, His angels are constantly watching over us. You don't need to have another sleepless night because of what the enemy is doing. Go to bed! Get a good night's rest; sleep well! For He that covers you has all in control.

Let no one deprive you of your rest! Let no one steal your joy! Let no one rob you of your peace! Let no one stop your praise! God says to tell you,

> *"Lift up your heads, O ye gates; and be ye lift up, ye everlasting doors; and the King of glory shall come in"* -
> Psalm 24:9

You need to call Him into your situation. Let Him know that you need His divine intervention; then take a moment to praise and worship your God.

These strange battles require a special kind of response. You can't curse; you can't fight physically or verbally because the persons attacking you are also baptized in Jesus' name. They might even be filled with the Holy Ghost, which makes them a part of the body of Christ. You cannot war against your own body! Strange battle indeed! Those who are seeking your demise speak in tongues just like you; they eat with you, although they hate you. Strange warfare!

They attend the same church you do; ride on the same bus; in the same car or maybe the same taxi. You could even be walking, talking and laughing together. They take the Lord's Supper with you; wash your feet and dry it but behind your back, they work witchcraft just to get you out so they can take your place. Strange battles in strange places!

Did that shock you? I hope not. It is the truth! Many leaders and aspirant leaders face these battles daily, right in the church. There are strange battles going on, from the pulpit to the pew. They throw stones at you, but you cannot retaliate. "So, what am I going to do?" you ask. Do like David; pray and praise your way through. They kick the dust of your past into your face and you are overcome with humiliation. Do not retaliate by trying to expose them. Instead declare, "I am in but I am on my way out!"

Stand in your authority as an anointed servant of the Most High God and prophesy, "He will not suffer my foot to be moved. My keeper does not slumber nor sleep. The Lord is my keeper." Place your hand on yourself and be the prophet over you own life. Speak to your ministry, your gifts, your calling and your destiny. I know Absalom wants to get you out! I know Shimei has capitalized on the situation and has publicly disgraced you. But encourage yourself in the Lord.

Declare, "The Lord is my keeper. The Lord is my shade upon my right hand." I know that you are not under this attack because you have wronged anyone. I see that these are anointed enemies. I know that the reason they have conspired to destroy you is to take your position in the body of Christ. I know that the war is as a result of covetousness. I know you did not call yourself but was chosen by God. Now you are under a strange attack in a strange place. But do not despair; He who called you is near!

God saw me in my undone condition and decided to place this anointing on me. I did not go seeking it. I was occupied with my own worldly ambitions, when He laid His nail-scarred hands on me. He took me from the pit; anointed me and placed me in the pulpit. Your story may not be the same as mine but I am sure He has done some work on you too.

I did nothing to get this anointing. I did not ask for this anointing. I did nothing to be me! So why then can't you stand to see me? Why can't you stand to see the sister or brother? What did they do to you?

God wants me to let you who are being ostracized because of His anointing on your life know: **This battle is not yours! This one is on God!** David used the sword, spear, sling, bow and arrow in many battles. However, for this battle, none of those weapons are appropriate to defeat this enemy.

This battle is so different, you need to keep the information you have within your belly; you will need to hold it all inside. This cannot be disclosed to your best friend. It must remain as classified information, lest you share it and those close to you do not understand. To try to explain this to someone could result in you being misunderstood.

God sent me to tell you that He is asking you to give the situation to Him. Say, **"Lord, this one is on You! I won't fight back. I won't retaliate in any way. I lift mine eyes and look to You. All of my help comes from You! Lord I will praise my way out of this one! I will trust You and watch You handle this situation."**

The witchcraft that is on you; the pressure that you are experiencing is from persons whom you love and respect. They have turned their backs on you. They have totally rejected you and have risen against you for no known reason at all, at all, at all!

God says, *"Don't worry! I am going to fight this battle for you and whenever it is over, no one will be able to point a finger at you. No one can say that you have avenged yourself. God says that He is going to take the enemy by the head. "I am going to swing him by the head," says the Lord. "When I am through defeating the enemy no one will be able to accuse you of wrong doing or vengeance. I am fighting this battle for you!"* saith God.

God says that He is delivering you from this strange warfare. He says that this one is on Him; He is fighting for you and He is breaking the curse! Hallelujah! Lift your hands and shout the name of 'Jesus' three times and watch God break the curse, fight the battle and destroy the yoke! Hallelujah! It is done! Glory!

David asked, "Why are my enemies increased?" He pointed out that since this strange battle erupted, enemies emerged from all angles. But David said, "Lord, I was young and now I am old and I have never seen the righteous forsaken." God's promise is that He will never forsake you. You are anointed to overcome this!

I hear the Holy Ghost calling your name! God says that your moment has come for elevation! The Lord is going to fix the situation in your home. Today is the day of deliverance! Hallelujah! Come on warriors! Today is the day of deliverance from this strange warfare! God will deliver you from all the persons who backbite and later smile with you, as well as those who kiss and betray you.

Lift up those sanctified hands toward heaven and praise your way out! God says that He is going to intervene in your situation. I see witchcraft in homes, turning husbands against their wives, resulting in separation. God says that today, He is dealing with that attack! It is coming from the Absalom spirit. It does not like to see what you have and wants to take it from you. But God says that He is dealing with that today!

Raise those hands warriors! Call on the name of Jesus and watch Him fix it! God says that this one is on Him! "I am fighting this strange battle that has risen up against you", says the Lord. Hallelujah! Get ready warriors! Now! Now! Now! It is time to get radical and declare, WAR!!! WAR!!! WAR!!! We are WARRING UNCLEAN SPIRITS!!!

We are fighting battles in strange places! We are in unexpected warfare! Persons who you thought would be supporting you are the very ones risen up against you. Get ready! God says, "Do not curse; bless them that curse you. Do not fight back; turn the other cheek." The Lord says that you should stand still and watch the deliverance that He is about to give to you.

Do nothing but worship and praise! I repeat, do nothing but worship and praise! Speak to yourself: "I am not going to fight. I won't get on the cell-phone and tear down anyone. I will worship and praise the Lord. I will be still and watch Him fix the situation."

God says that He honours and respects your faith. The distance you have come by faith, has caught His attention and He will be giving you a shift in your situation. Are you ready for the move of God? All you need, God will provide. The devil is a liar!

The devil has blocked you but the Holy Ghost says, "NO!" The devil is a liar. Shout the name of Jesus and say, "Hands off devil! I will go where God wants me to go!" Believe that God is doing it right now! The curse is broken in Jesus name! Push back witchcraft, right now! Push it back! Push it back! Reverse the curse warriors; reverse it in Jesus name! There is an anointing to break witchcraft present; tap into it with your worship and your praise.

This is a prophetic word for someone reading this book. God is going to heal you from the sickness caused through that attack. He is destroying that yoke right now too! Whatever was thrown into your yard and you stepped over it, is affecting you. You are fighting a strange battle but God is delivering you from that, right now! Just shout the name of Jesus; your breakthrough is here! Be loosed, right now! Be delivered in the mighty name of Jesus!

An anointing is flowing right now warriors to destroy the spirit of Absalom that is affecting your life and ministry. Leaders, you can't sit back and play dead, while the devil takes your health, wealth, family, business, ministry, gifts or your calling. Get in the Holy Ghost and speak to the situation.

God has released a word of victory in the midst of these strange battles. But you have to receive it by faith and praise your way out. The nature of the attack is irrelevant, so too is the strategy. God says that the battle is His and the victory is yours; so do not wait until it is over, shout now! Whether it is witchcraft, sorcery, necromancy, de Laurence, lodge, black magic or any other form of evil, affecting your life, the anointing is here to break it!

Regardless of the hindrance causing the block in your life and resulting in you going around in circles, God says that today is your day! It is true that the attacks are coming through people you least expect but shift your focus from the enemy, place it on Jesus. Raise your hands and begin to worship God and watch the dynamics shift.

Yes! Strange battles have emerged in strange places against you. They are propelled by covetousness and the devil is coming to steal, kill and destroy. But the devil is a liar! The Spirit of Almighty God raises up a standard against every foul and unclean spirit militating these attacks today. Praise God! Praise your way from the tail to the head; from the victim to the victor; from beneath to above; from lack to overflow; from war to peace; from sadness to joy; from hatred to love! Praise Him as He shifts the dynamics!

When you worship you pull down the glory. Warriors must heed the instructions of their commander in chief in each combat. For the strange battles in strange places, the instruction is to praise your way out! The Lord says that this one will not require engaging the enemy in any way, shape or form. This one requires only that you stand still and watch the salvation of the Lord. The enemies you see today, God says that you will see them again, no more!

That is ultimate victory! Praise the One who gave it to you! His name is Jesus!

The body of Christ needs leaders who are anointed; leaders who can see what the enemy is doing and can watch over their congregation. The level of anointing in the house should make preaching and prophesying easy. The level of praise and worship, along with the anointing on the leader are prime indicators of the level to which the power of God will manifest.

People are experiencing attacks of all kinds and turn to the church for help. While the Lord is fighting for us as leaders; we on the other hand, are expected to be equipped and operating in an atmosphere created for the Spirit of God to flow through us to bring healing and deliverance. Sinners will be loosed from every mind-binding and will-blocking spirits and surrender their lives to Jesus Christ; taking on the name of Jesus in water baptism.

The atmosphere needs to be one through which angels walk to do God's bidding because it is fully charged with the anointing. Wherever this does not exist, desperate people of God will begin to gravitate towards other congregations where help, healing and restoration are being experienced. Leaders are supposed to be open to the operation of the five-fold ministry in their church. If you are not, then when members leave your church, it is more likely an act of desperation for help and not dishonour.

No one except those carrying the spirit of Absalom, Miriam, Cain, Judas, Ham, Jezebel and Ahab will come into an atmosphere fully charged with the anointing where they are being ministered to by someone who is truly anointed and leave without experiencing the manifestation of the power of God in one way or another. The aforementioned are usually untouched because their dishonouring and undermining spirits hinder them from being able to tap into the anointing of the leader who they are against.

Chapter Six

The Ultimate Example of the Leader Who Covers

Love is the key!

1Corinthians 13:

> *Though I speak with the tongues of men and of angels, and have not charity, I am become as sounding brass, or a tinkling cymbal.*
>
> *And though I have the gift of prophecy, and understand all mysteries, and all knowledge; and though I have all faith, so that I could remove mountains, and have not charity, I am nothing.*
>
> *And though I bestow all my goods to feed the poor, and though I give my body to be burned and have not charity, it profiteth me nothing.*
>
> *Charity suffereth long, and is kind; charity envieth not; charity vaunteth not itself, is not puffed up,*
>
> *Doth not behave itself unseemly, seeketh not her own, is not easily provoked, thinketh no evil;*

Rejoiceth not in iniquity, but rejoiceth in the truth;

Beareth all things, believeth all things, hopeth all things, endureth all things.

Charity never faileth: but whether there be prophecies, they shall fail; whether there be tongues, they shall cease; whether there be knowledge, it shall vanish away,

For we know in part and prophesy in part.

But when that which is perfect is come, then that which is in part shall be done away.

When I was a child, I spake as a child, I understood as a child, I thought as a child: but when I became a man, I put away childish things.

For now we see through a glass, darkly; but then face to face: now I know in part; but then shall I know even as also I am known.

And now abideth faith, hope, charity, these three; but the greatest of these is charity.

Of the three most powerful weapons, charity, which is godly love, is the greatest. Indeed the greatest weapon the world has ever seen is love. United we stand and divided we fall.

I have strict instructions for you before closing this message from the Lord to the leader who covers. This is the Law of Christ that you love your neighbor as yourself. Disobedience is sin. I repeat, this is the Law of Christ, that you love your neighbour as yourself. You would do nothing to harm yourself because you love yourself; so love your neighbour!

Love is the most powerful weapon! This is the weapon that God uses against His enemies. When Lucifer turned against the Almighty God, he began to point accusatory fingers at God and those angels that chose to remain on God's side. When he did this, God could have destroyed them all (Lucifer and the one third of the stars who took side with him) in a flash but instead God used love. God is love!

The bible did not say that God 'exousia'; but tells us that GOD IS LOVE! God displays love as explained in the popular bible verse, John 3:16:

> *For God so loved the world, that He 'gave' His only begotten Son.*

Love gives! So the first characteristic of love is 'giving'. God displayed His love by giving His only begotten Son. When God wanted a family in the earth; when He wanted sons, He gave His only Son.

That is a principle – as long as the earth remains, whatever you sow, that is what you will reap. That is a universal principle –SEED TIME AND HARVEST TIME. God wants sons, so He gave a Son. God wanted a family, so He sowed like Abraham, who was to become the father of a great nation. He too, first had to give his only begotten son. God says, you need children Abraham, you first have to give. Love is giving!

As I began looking at the life of Christ, my attention was drawn to Paul's writing in 1st Corinthians 13, which is referred to as the 'Love Chapter'. An in-depth look at the book of Corinthians will reveal that chapter 12 as well as chapter 14 speaks of the gifts of the Spirit. However, just between the gift chapters, Paul placed the 'Love Chapter'. This is by divine inspiration. The message is that the "gifts" will not be balanced without love. It is love that balances the gifts of the Spirit. Without Love you will not function effectively. Love is the strength, the foundation, and love is definitely the secret for the church.

I want you to understand that Jesus came at a very critical time in church history. The bible says that Jesus came 'when the fullness of time was come.' This means that God waited on the appointed time; the right time; the fullness of time was come. God sent forth His Son, being made of a woman, made under the law to redeem them who were under the law. So He was here when the law was in force.

The law was the schoolmaster; it was the Pedagogue. The law was that schoolgirl who brought people to Christ. When Jesus showed up, His mandate was to bring an end to that system. That is what the word 'fulfilled' means –accomplished, bring to an end. I want you to understand here that Jesus walked under the law but His mission was to start a new era – a new system; to release a fresh move. While He was here, He obeyed everything the Law commanded. However, even though He obeyed everything which the Law commanded, He came to bring that system to an end because the Law was limited and carried a string.

On His final day in the flesh; His very last day as a human in the earth; the last day of His Ministry on earth, the bible tells us that this was the day before the feast of the Passover. Jesus knew that His hour was come. It was time for Him to depart the world and return unto His Father. He declared how much he had loved His own which were in the world. He loved them even unto the end.

The bible says that He sat with them and partook in the feast of the Passover although He was the Passover lamb. He sat with them and began to eat the bread of the Passover, however the bread that He was eating signified His flesh that would be broken for us. The wine from the grapevine that He drank, signified the blood that He was about to shed, a few hours later. He sat there knowing very well that those were His final hours on earth.

As He sat there, He questioned what should be His last words to them. What shall I say to them so that they can remember after I am gone and rehearse as my final words? Whenever someone is about to die, if they call to speak with you, their final words are always the most important words. This is because mankind has a proclivity to 'save the best for last'. Here Jesus knowing that His hour had come, sat and ate with His disciples.

At the end of the supper, Satan put it in the heart of Judas Iscariot (Simon's son) to betray Jesus. He said that the Father had given all things into His hands and that He was come from God and that He would be going back to God. Jesus is God giving of Himself. He is the expressed image of God - the visible manifestation of the invisible God. He is the unseen who came on the scene to be seen. He is God giving Himself in flesh. Jesus is God wrapped up in flesh. He is the Father incarnate. He is God manifested to take away the sins of the world so He came from God.

That same Jesus, rose from supper, took a towel and girded Himself. This was His final hour and He wanted to leave an indelible mark on the lives of His followers. It had to be something that would stay with them as long as they remained on the earth. Jesus took off His outer garments, which is indicative of Him now revealing Himself. Here He exposed Himself to His disciples. He poured water into a basin and began to wash His disciples' feet. Thereafter, He wiped them with the towel with which He had girded Himself.

This calls for a pause at this juncture, because, according to Judaism, masters do not wash servants' feet. Jesus was living under a system that put segregation between people. He was living in a system where those who were non-Jews could not enter into the temple. They would have to stay at the outer court. He was living in a system where a woman faces certain restrictions because of her gender. In that culture, the woman could not divorce her husband but the man had the power to write a letter of divorcement for any reason – as simple as burning the pot. As a woman, you could not be a priest; you were forbidden to handle anything that is beyond the third dimension of the temple and you were so restricted!

Jesus, therefore, lived in an era where a servant did not have the privilege to readily walk into his master's bedroom. If you were a servant, you could not have sat at the masters' table. As long as you were poor, you did not have the privilege to walk into your master's chamber or bedroom and sit with his guests. You were required to keep out! There were barriers; so Jesus came to fix that which Adam messed up.

If you were not a Jew, you could not have been a priest neither could you have been a prophet. As long as you were not of the tribe of Levi, you could not walk with the incense and give it to God in the temple. God declared in His word: "Israel, you only have I chosen of all the families of the earth." God referred to everybody else as 'dogs' and 'sorcerers'. If you belonged to Israel, you were considered royal priesthood, everybody else was considered 'nothing'. They were therefore not privileged to come before God. Jews, were a peculiar people; special to God.

Jesus then entered the scene, lived under the Jewish system which segregated mankind. He lived under the system that belittled women and even belittled those who were paralyzed. The system stated that if you were born with eleven fingers, you were forbidden to go into the temple. It was a system which dictated that if you had any kind of deformity you could not present yourself before God. In that system you were considered a 'nobody'. Jesus' final hours on earth began revealing something that was different from the religion of the fore-fathers. He took a towel and a basin, poured water in the basin and began washing His disciples' feet.

Within that ere, after you walked the streets wearing sandals on those dusty roads, your feet would be covered with dust and dirt. On arriving home, the servants would immediately wash their masters' feet. That is the office of the 'no good' or the 'no body'. Then came Jesus, the Master; the Lord of all; the Creator; the God who said, "Let there be light." He took off His priestly garment, took a towel and basin with water and was now washing His disciples' feet. He washed some of the others and eventually got to Simon Peter.

Peter said unto Him, "Lord you have to stop right here!" I am not going to allow you to wash my feet because I know that according to our Jewish law and customs, Masters do not wash their servants' feet and Lord, You are the only one around town who opened Your mouth and commanded the leper to be cleansed and it was done. You are the only One, who when the paralyzed came before You, at Your command, he was made whole. You are the only One who spoke to one who had been dead for four days and he came back to life."

Peter continued, "Lord it is I who confessed that You are the Christ. I declared that You are the Seed of David. I confessed that you are Jehovah our salvation. I declared that You are Immanuel – God with us! So how come you want me to allow You, God to wash my feet? My feet? No way! You will never wash my feet for that would be disrespectful!"

Jesus said unto him, "What I do now Peter, You do not know, but you shall know hereafter because Peter, I know you have never seen it like this. I know you are familiar, with the doctrines of the fore-fathers. You are familiar with how the scribes operate; whenever they go anywhere, they washed their feet and hands. You observe and have knowledge of how the scribes react if anyone touched them whenever they visited the market place. They wash themselves! You know of the operations of the Pharisees too; how pious they are and how they viewed the common people as nothing. So Peter, what I am doing, you do not understand as yet. I am here to start a new movement and to establish the kingdom of God."

Peter said "Sir, You shall never wash my feet, I will never debase You nor allow You to condescend to my level." But Jesus answered him saying, "If I wash thee not, thou hath no part with me."

Can you imagine how dumbfounding this was for Peter? He genuinely thought that he was doing the right thing and that his actions proved that he respected Jesus above the rest. But now Jesus was blowing His mind when He explained to Peter that in the system that He was setting up, if one does not humble himself and become a servant, he will have no part in His kingdom.

Did you hear that? You have no part in the kingdom of God, unless you humble yourself. You have to forget about your position in life. You have to forget what you have acquired and your family background. Now God is here in flesh; He is better than all of us because He is God! Yet He made Himself of no reputation and took on the form of man and became a servant. God says to tell you that if you do not wash your neighbour's feet, you have no lot nor part with Him. This is a question to ask your neighbour within the body of Christ. Neighbour, will you wash my feet? Will you remove the dirt from me? Will you help me to get rid of the mess that I have picked up? On life's journey, we all pick up some stuff. Will you humble yourself and wash off that which I have picked up?

I have news for you! Leaders, aspiring leaders and fellow citizens of the kingdom of God, if you do not wash your neighbours' feet, you will have no lot nor part with the new move that Jesus initiated. A shift was about to take place. Peter would not be left out, so he said in humility, "Here are my feet Lord; wash them! Do you want to wash my hands too? Here they are! Do you want to wash my face too? Here, take it Jesus!"

Jesus told him, "No! No! That is for baptism and this demonstration is not about baptism. This is about you, forgetting about yourselves when you come to church." In the body of Christ, you are not better than me and I am not better than you. Don't let your car, house, or the amount of money you have in the bank fool you.

Let it blow Holy Spirit, blow in Your house! Blow in Your house! Jesus said,

> *"You call me Master, you call me Lord and you say well, for so I am. Well if I then be your Master and Lord have washed your feet, you also ought to wash each other's feet.*

If Jesus looked beyond your faults and saw your needs, you then need to look beyond my faults and see my needs. That is covering the anointing. If God forgave you, then you should forgive me. That is the message for all the warriors.

Some do not know what real church is all about; this is real church! Jesus said, for I have given you an example that you should follow. As I have done to you, so you should do to others. He said,

> "Verily, verily, I say unto you that the servant is not greater than his master, neither is He that is sent, greater than He that sent him. If you know these things, happy are you if you do them."

Come on leaders, if you want joy or real happiness, then you need to find someone with dirty feet and wash them. Do you really want joy believers? Then whatever you do to me, you would really have done it to yourselves. If you want joy as a leader, find someone to cover! Jesus said, I speak not of you all. Jesus was saying that this principle is for those whom He has chosen.

That word 'chosen' requires attention, because the word 'church' really does not refer to a building. It is from the Greek word 'ecclesia' which means 'the chosen' or 'called out' ones. Jesus is therefore saying that He knows His church; He knows those whom He has called. The fact that He was eating bread and drinking with one who was going to lift up his heel against Him, was merely for the fulfilling of the scripture.

You, therefore, need to understand what church is. Not everyone in the 'church' will love you. Judas is in the church! They will walk with you, talk with you and stab you in the back. They will tell you how much they love you, kiss you until your jaw becomes raw and then betray you like Judas. Don't try to rid yourself of Judas!

To the natural man, it is inconceivable that this was Jesus' last day on the earth and Judas was still with Him after three and a half years, unexposed! Can you imagine, the enemy was in His midst all this time? Jesus knew the enemy but did not expose him. I want you to know that you do not have to do anything to your enemy. Let them be! You do not have to kill Judas. He will purchase his own rope! Yes, Judas will hang himself! You do not have to do anything at all, at all, at all!

Jesus continued to speak

"Now I tell you before it come, that, when it came to pass, ye may believe that I am He" John 13:19

Again, this statement blows my mind because Jesus said that at that time the apostles will know that 'I am *he*.' Look at the word '*he*' in your bibles. It is placed in italics by the translators. This means that it was not in the original Greek scriptures but was placed there by the translators. Jesus did not say "In that day you shall know that I am *he*", instead He said, "In that day ye shall know that I am."

He was identifying Himself with the 'I am' who visited Moses in the burning bush. Jesus said "In that day, ye will know that I am the I am that I am. Come on now, don't get it twisted, Jesus is God! Yes He is God! Jesus told the apostles that after that night season was over, a new day would dawn. When that day dawned, they would not have to ask who the Father is. In that day, they would realize that, it is the Father that spoke whenever Jesus spoke. In that day, they would realize that in seeing Jesus, they were seeing and hearing the Father.

God is about to do something in your life as a leader! This is a prophetic word. God is about to do something in your life! I reiterate, it is prophetic, so you will need to take it.

I often share with my congregation that I have a love for cologne. I tell them that I am a cologne specialist. One day someone came to me with a message from an officer. He said the officer told him to let me know that he is now selling colognes. He made mention of a particular cologne and said to tell me that he had that one. The person, who brought the message, asked how the officer knew what cologne I used. Another individual in my midst responded that there are persons who are cologne specialists.

If you know the fragrance of Grey Flannel or Bleu De Chanel, wherever you go and those fragrances are being used, you will readily identify them. The fragrance is in the atmosphere. I told them that as a cologne specialist, I know how to spray cologne. Ok now, do not allow a covetous spirit to cause you to miss the message. There is a deeper truth to what I am sharing so stick with me. There are different techniques in spraying cologne. A specialist will not place the cologne too close to their clothes as this will not yield the full fragrance of the cologne.

There is a technique called 'whiplash' where the cologne is placed six to twelve inches away from the user before spraying. There is a second technique called 'carpet spraying'. This procedure involves, turning the cologne upside down and releasing it in the air. The user then opens his arms and walks under the mist.

You need to get wise now! There is a word over your head. It is up to you to receive or reject it. You may go ahead and keep quiet but someone is about to step out and walk underneath this word. God is about to change your season! Your night season is about to close and God is about to bring about the dawn of a new day! Open your mouth and declare: My day! My day! My day is about to dawn!

God is about to give me a fresh move. Whenever God is about to change your season, this is what He does: He takes someone from your life! So whenever they begin to curse you; speak evil of you; backbite or stop contacting you regularly on the phone, do not cry nor wonder why. Do you not realize that God is about to change your season?

Notice also that whenever God is about to protect you, He removes somebody from your life. Whenever He is going to bless you, He adds someone to your life. God is about to release your butler in your life! Your Boaz is about to show up! Do not compromise! Do not betray the anointing! Stand flat-footed!

It is all about Jesus! He is about to flip the script! God is about to turn your mourning into dancing! Hallelujah! He is about to remove death and bring life. Glory be to God! Speak over your life right now: Change! Change! Go ahead and worship God for your new season! Open your mouth and declare it: New season! New season!

In your endeavour to be a leader who covers, I know that you have encountered much pain, shame and dishonour. I know that you have engaged in many strange warfare. Yes, you could have retaliated and exposed those who abused and sought to destroy you, but instead you obeyed God's instructions and covered them. God saw it and is about to reward you! Go ahead and praise Him for the new season He is about to release in your life and ministry.

Chapter Seven

Follow the Leader Who Covers

Learn this!

If you do not wish to remember everything I have written so far, be sure to retain this word of wisdom. This is for everyone who God will be using in His kingdom in these end times. Absalom and Solomon had the same father-David. Absalom viewed his father as a murderer and an adulterer but Solomon hailed him as the greatest man the earth had ever seen. Solomon revered his father as the Lord's anointed.

God seeing the heart of Solomon instructed David to empty out himself into Solomon. God told David to pass on the anointing he carried onto Solomon before he went to sleep with his fathers. There is no benefit in David taking it to the grave with him; but God will never raise up those who conspire against and slaughter their leader.

The leader that covers shall reap the glory of the risen Christ. I have learnt this, that whatever you honour will gravitate to you and whatever you dishonour will withdraw from you. Honour attracts while dishonour, repels. That is why God says in His words,

"He that humbleth himself shall be exalted."

God will draw them to Him! Hallelujah!

If you want God to raise you up, do not 'sell out'-betray- the members within the body of Christ. Instead choose to cover them. Can God still find leaders who are willing to cover each other and the flock which He has anointed them to cover? Are there still believers whose resolve is to cover and not go against leaders and others within the household of faith?

If you are, I want you to make this declaration: **"I am going to fulfill God's command to bear one another's burden."**

As a young believer, I was at the altar one night; kneeling beside me was a sister, praying. I am confessing here that I eavesdropped on her prayer. What she said, remains with me until this very day! She stuck her tongue out and cried, "Jesus! Jesus! Mi tongue a put mi inna trouble! Jesus! Si mi tongue yah! Please step pan eh Jesus!"

I think it would be one of the wisest prayer believers with a similar problem could pray. Some believers' ministries are being blocked like Miriam's because of their tongue. She 'chat' too much! It led her to dishonour Moses by daring to rebuke him, God's anointed. It was her tongue that stopped the word released over her life from being fulfilled.

I have news for someone and I want you to keep this word with you. Never forget this! NO ONE CAN STOP THE CHURCH! NO ONE CAN BLOCK YOUR ANOINTING! No witchcraft or evil minds can hinder you from reaping the good of the land which God has promised you. CHECK YOUR TONGUE! CHECK YOUR TONGUE! It is the only weapon that can hinder you and it is your responsibility to control it.

Many who have died; many eating from garbage bins; many who are out of Christ, are where they are because of words which were released from their own mouths. God says that each of us as Christians should place a bridle on our tongue. One, who is unable to control his tongue, will not inherit that which God has in store for him.

The vast majority of persons, who die violently, in an untimely manner, did so because of words which emanated from their own mouths. Many of you reading this book have great ministries within you. However, unless you learn how to control your tongue, you will never manifest your gifts.

The gifts are not given to draw attention to yourself. They are given to bring glory and honour to God who gave them. Those desirous of getting attention want gifts to become famous. Their motive is to become popular. I have news for you as well: you are falling right into the trap of the devil!

It is not usually long before a close examination will reveal that most persons, who desire to be powerful, crave this for self-gratification. God is saying that He cannot and will never trust those individuals. Whenever these persons are tested, they display a wrong spirit; which consequently disqualifies them from receiving a greater anointing from the Lord.

God is definitely pouring out His Spirit on believers in these last days as He promised in Joel 2 but He will not release that yoke breaking, burden removing anointing on a leader who refuses to cover. It is time for us to come into agreement with God and each other! There is going to be a supernatural outpouring of the anointing on believers within the body of Christ. God says that He is taking the church to another level.

There is far too much tearing-down among believers, including leaders. God says that too many people within the church are speaking ill of each other. The dishonouring of the bishops, elders, evangelists, missionaries, choristers, deacons, ushers, musicians, technicians, sisters and brothers has grieved God and He is calling us to repentance. He wants us to make a change! God says that it is time for a shift! He needs believers who are committed to covering each other and bearing each other's burdens.

We are coming in agreement with God and each other so that the prophets, prophetesses, Shems, gifts of healing, gifts of miracle, callings and divine purpose for believers will be released. God says that He can only trust those who will cover one another; those who will fast and pray for each other; those who are willing to help each other; those who know how to lift each other up and those who are willing to keep watch over each other's souls.

There are some sad truths about the church. It is the only army that fights against itself. It is also the only army that leaves its wounded soldiers to die on the battlefield. As a leader, God has called me to cover His people and I use this medium to beseech all leaders and believers in general to do the same.

I am committed to covering you!

We are given the whole armour of God to cover ourselves in Ephesians 6:13-17:

> *Wherefore take unto you the whole armour of God, that ye may be able to withstand in the evil day, and having done all, to stand.*
>
> *Stand therefore, having your loins girt about with truth, and having on the breastplate of righteousness;*
>
> *And your feet shod with the preparation of the gospel of peace;*
>
> *Above all, taking the shield of faith, wherewith ye shall be able to quench all the fiery darts of the wicked.*
>
> *And take the helmet of salvation, and the sword of the Spirit, which is the word of God*

The fundamental truth in Christian warfare is:

> *We wrestle not against flesh and blood, but against principalities, against powers, against the rulers of darkness of this world, against spiritual wickedness in high places v12.*

Now watch this! There is helmet for your head; breastplate for your chest; belt for your waist; shoe for your feet; shield for various parts of your body and a sword to be on the offensive or defensive. But there is absolutely nothing for your back! The back of each warrior is exposed; open to the enemy and renders you an easy target for destruction if you are fleeing from the enemy.

God says that there is one protection for the backs of Christian warriors- other warriors who cover! Each believer is expected to cover the back of the other believer. Yes! I have your back and you have mine! God says that I need to protect you and you need to protect me. God says to tell you that He chose you to cover the back of your neighbour. In so doing, we will all be covered. In Jamaican dialect, I am your 'backitive' and you are mine.

Arm yourself with the sword of the Spirit, the word of God and let us get on the offensive. Let us unite in warring unclean spirits that are coming up against us in the church. There are some backbiting, tale bearing, gossiping spirits that want to 'backstab' believers. They are after the leaders as well as the officers and members of the church. But we declare war against them in the name of Jesus.

We speak Isaiah 54:17 over each other's life:

> *No weapon that is formed against thee shall prosper; and every tongue that shall rise against thee in judgment thou shalt condemn.*

Prophesy over your life too:

> *The LORD is my light and my salvation; whom shall I fear? The LORD is the strength of my life; of whom shall I be afraid?*
> *When the wicked, even mine enemies and my foes, came upon me to eat up my flesh, they stumbled and fell.*
> *Though an host should encamp against me, my heart shall not fear: though war should rise against me, in this will I be confident.*

One thing have I desired of the Lord, that will I seek after; that I may dwell in the house of the LORD all the days of my life, to behold the beauty of the LORD, and to enquire in His temple.

For in the time of trouble He shall hide me in His pavilion: in the secret of His tabernacle shall He hide me; He shall set me upon a rock.

And now shall mine head be lifted up above mine enemies round about me: therefore will I offer sacrifices of joy; I will sing, yea, I will sing praises unto the LORD. Psalm 27:1-6.

Plea the blood of Jesus against the plans of the enemy coming against your life; as well as the lives of your fellow warriors in Christ. Lift up that wounded soldier, place him on your back and carry him to safety. Let us commit ourselves to saving the wounded soldiers in God's army. There is a hurting brother and a sister in pain, don't pass them. Come on! Let us bear each other up!

The race is not for the swift, nor the battle for the strong. It is a race of endurance. Today, you might be operating in full strength while someone else is weak. But tomorrow, who knows, you might be weak and need someone to carry you.

Carry someone in prayer!

Carry someone in fasting!

Carry someone with an encouraging word!

Carry someone by sowing a tangible seed in their life to meet an obvious need!

Remember that whatsoever you sow, that will you also reap. I am sowing a covering anointing! I cover you right now in the name of Jesus. I cover you in faith, believing that as I cover you God is releasing an anointing on someone to cover me.

I cover you from the enemy!

I cover you from bad mind!

I cover you from covetousness!

I cover you from obeah-witchcraft!

I cover you from bitterness!

I cover you from hatred!

Yes! I feel the anointing of God, covering you right this very minute. I feel the anointing pushing back the enemy; pushing back the haters right now! Cover! Cover! Cover! God is raising up leaders who cover! God is raising up an army in which soldiers cover each other.

This is a rhema word from God! It is time for us to cover! I cover you; you cover me. Let the person you are covering know that they will not backslide; they are not leaving the church. Reassure them with your covering that they are coming out of whatever the devil has them in. Tell somebody:

You are coming out! You are coming out! You are coming out!

You are coming out with power! You are coming out with gifts!

You are coming out with a new anointing!

Shoot down everything the enemy has released against the body of Christ!

Release a missile of a unified praise and worship in the camp of the enemy and shoot down every prince demon attacking leaders, ministries and the body of Christ in general! Bear one another's burden and so fulfill the law of Christ. I choose to cover the believers in the body of Christ. I declare it: I am a leader who covers!

I have options, but I choose to cover! I promise to pray for you! I promise to fast for you! I hide you under the blood of Jesus. In an atmosphere where we cover each other, there is power! Let your brothers and sisters in Christ know that you are covering them. Let your leaders know that you are covering them.

Cover them from every known attack: Bad mind, covetousness, hatred, bitterness, accidents, hypertension, diabetes, insanity, nervous disorders, mental illnesses, HIV/AIDS, heart diseases and any other form of attack.

The impact of this change will reach far beyond our individual ministries and churches. It is going to spiral to our homes, work places, communities and schools until it transforms our nation. This is the ultimate transformational leadership style, designed and modeled by the Creator Himself, Jesus Christ! It requires a personal decision, to be a leader who covers!

What is your decision? I trust it is one to cover.

Jesus left these important words with His disciples in John 13:34 as He explained that in the Jewish law there were six hundred and thirteen commandments, rules and regulations. However He came to begin a new move; *A new commandment I give unto you, That ye love one another; as I have loved you, that ye also should love one another.*

In like manner, this new commandment is now given to leaders who cover. It is the same word that Jesus left with the disciples who were the world leaders and changers in their time. Today, this is the same word from God for all leaders and aspiring leaders within the body of Christ: **Love one another**.

He says,

> *"By this, all men will know that you are my disciples, if you love one another."*

We need more love! That is what we need in the church. You need to love me and I need to love you. I am making reference here to **agape love** – godly love. You need to love me if you desire the move of God in your life.

You cannot be selfish and experience the glory! God is getting ready to release something awesome within the body of Christ in this season. But love is the key to unlocking this move in the church. Love opens every door! It is the commandment that was a shadow in the Old Testament. Only a few men in the Old Testament were moved by love. Love covers! Love honours!

David was mentioned earlier as possessing a spirit that honours the anointing. The reason no devil could kill him before his time, was that he manifested the love of God. This is lacking in the churches. I say this without apology! There is far too much segregation and partiality among churches. A number of our church leaders conduct the affairs of the church with favouritism and discrimination. If one attends the church and holds what is considered a prestigious job, after six months he is selected as an officer in the church. This creates a division in most churches.

Someone who is impoverished, uneducated or is not influential, is considered as 'nothing' in some of our churches. This is a blatant disregard for Jesus' command. It is not so with the kingdom of God. For this reason, I ensure that every person attending our church is offered a warm, healthy meal, without discrimination and free of cost on Sundays. We want love to abide in the church! I need to be able to feed you and you must be able to feed me. We ought to be touched with the feelings of each other's infirmities. We need more love! More love! More love! If I am at home and hungry, there ought to be someone in the church who is able to sense that I have such need. Likewise, one must be able to feel my pressure and groan in the spirit for me.

This message must be released as this book comes to its close. I know you might get somewhat uncomfortable if you do not love your brethren like you should. I must release this word nonetheless. I say repeatedly, that no one has the power to hinder me from speaking as the Holy Spirit gives me utterance. I know I offend sometimes. But by now, those familiar with me will know that I am not a regular sermonic preacher who is meticulous in articulating. I am rough and rugged! I carry a John the Baptist and Elijah spirit. I carry fire! And the more you try to sit on the word, the more God wants me to release it! The more you try to ignore it, is the more determined I am to ensure that it is released to the glory of God.

I repeat: This is a clarion call! I will echo it until the body of Christ comes into agreement with this message and begin to declare it too. WE NEED MORE LOVE!

How can I come to church, sit, praise God until the service dismisses and then leave the church grounds without greeting even one person? Ironically, these are the same persons who complain that there is no love in the church. You are the ones who have no love! Remember, whatsoever you sow, that shall you also reap. Go take another look! It is there in your bible. If you sow love, fellowship, and greeting; that shall you also reap.

It is time to get real radical within the body of Christ, if you want to experience God's end time move. Those who are more concerned about the leader's expository method of preaching or exegesis, take note of this: God said to Moses in Exodus 25:8

"And let them make me a tabernacle; that I may dwell among them.

In some translations it is referred to as tent. A look at the etymology of the word 'tabernacle' introduces you to a Hebrew word 'mishkan' which means residence or dwelling place. God says, build me a 'mishkan' and I will be your neighbour.

Build me a tabernacle and I will be your neighbour. That word 'mishkan' means indwelling – God says, build me 'mishkan' and I will dwell with you. The word 'mishkan' is the same root word in Hebrew for Shekinah glory and the same root word in Hebrew for 'Shakhen' is the same word for neighbour.

This is why Jesus asked the question: How can you say that you love God and hate your neighbour? God says that He will never be your neighbour if you refuse to love each other. So the word mishkan or Shekhina glory is God encamping with you – becoming your neighbour. The Shekinah glory is the 'neighbour spirit'. It only shows up in a building, community, or nation where there is love. It shows up whenever persons are in one accord. It shows up when you learn how to become a neighbour to their neighbour.

Whenever you begin to love the person next to you, the way you love yourself; then and only then can you cover them with agape love. God will send His neighbouring spirit and whenever it comes, it is accompanied by a glory. Jesus told His disciples to go to Jerusalem and wait on the 'neighbouring spirit' the Holy Ghost. They tarried for days without the Holy Ghost showing up. But the bible informs us that when they were in one place and finally in one accord, then SUDDENLY !!!!!

My neighbour, how you treat each other is a key factor in determining if you will receive 'A SUDDENLY!!!' The glory of God showing up in your life is dependent on whether you cover, love and honour one another. Can I talk to you up close and personal as I bring this book to a close?

Well! Well! Neighbour, you may sing all you want, preach like Paul, prophesy all the prophecies and know the bible from Genesis to Revelation. If you do not love your brother, you are nothing at all! At all! At all! A loud sounding brass or a tinkling cymbal; an empty barrel is what you are.

Neighbour, you've got to love me if you want the glory of God to show up in your life. If you want God to raise you up, you must treat your brother and sister right. You must forgive your brethren. Get radical and handle your business! Go ahead and do what needs to be done for the glory of God to manifest in your life, your ministry, your home, your community and by extension your country.

Neighbour, the glory of God will never come down until true praise goes up. My good neighbour, a true praise is a praise that comes from a true heart and a true heart is a heart that loves and covers. You cannot hate others, bite and devour them, then enter the sanctuary believing that your praises are going up to God. You cannot be expecting His glory to come down in a loveless atmosphere. The Shekinah glory is the 'neighbouring glory'.

I know that in some instances, you were really hurt, greatly ostracized and dishonoured. But Jesus reminded His children that the servant is not greater than the master. He said in John 15:20-21,

> *"Remember the word that I said unto you, The servant is not greater than his lord. If they have persecuted Me, they will also persecute you; if they have kept My saying, they will keep yours also.*
> *But all these things will they do unto you for My name's sake, because they know not Him that sent Me-God.*
> *He that hateth Me hateth My Father also.*

If Jesus had not come and spoken unto them, they would not know sin but because He did they have no cloak. Today! The word of the Lord to the body of Christ has been delivered. You have no excuse!

I reiterate, Jesus said, this is my new commandment:

> *that you love one another as I have loved you. Greater love has no man than this that a man lay down his life for his friend.*

Neighbour, God says this is the fundamental principle of the church. This is the foundation of the church. This is the rock upon which the church was established.

The church is different from Judaism. The church is different from religion and society. The church is the Rock of salvation. I love Luke 6:26-38,

> *Woe unto you when all men shall speak well of you! For so did their fathers to the false prophets.*

You see, if God really chose you, men will not speak well of you. You can know those who are called by God whenever you get into a taxi. If you are really a man of God, the world is going to hate you. Your own family will turn against you, if you really are a child of God.

Conversely, if you are a false prophet, the world will love you; while if you are a true prophet of God, the world is going to speak evil of you. Regardless, Jesus says,

> *"But I say unto you which hear, Love your enemies, do good to them which hate you."*

This is the church! The church does not hate its enemies. Some people only desire deliverance but do not really know what true church is all about. They go right back to the old dirty life after God delivers them. But whenever you are on Christ the solid Rock, old things are passed away and behold all things become new.

This is the new life! Do you know anyone who hates you? Do good to that person!

> *Bless them that curse you, and pray for them that despitefully use you.*

Let me repeat that: God says

> *"Bless them that curse you, and pray for them that despitefully use you."*

Is there anyone you know, who speaks evil of you? Well, your responsibility as a citizen of the kingdom of God and a member of the body of Christ, is to pray a good prayer for that individual. If you are unable to pray a good prayer, something is wrong with your heart. Your heart is still rock hard and God says that He wants to change that heart and give you one of flesh; one which can be touched with the feelings of the infirmities of others.

Like Jesus said:

"And unto him that smiteth thee on the one cheek offer also the other; and him that taketh away thy cloak, forbid not to take thy coat also."

This means that when you are dealing with that person who wants to hurt you, do not retaliate. I warn you not to fight back because whenever God is ready to take vengeance, He is really rough.

The enemy slaps you in the face and laughs but whenever God is repaying the enemy, jawbones become dislocated; cancer consumes the entire body and limbs becomes dismembered. Whenever, God is beating, that beating is from head to toe. Sicknesses which the doctors can neither diagnose nor cure begin to afflict the enemies.

So then, let God fight your battles. He will summon the rats and dispatch them into closets to devour entire wardrobes, including the newest pieces of clothing. He sends the palmer worm, the canker worm, the locust and the caterpillar. He will assign them to devour the enemy's finances. Children will begin to fall ill so frequently that even their life-savings are eroded.

God romps rough! And He says vengeance is mine; I will repay. So if the enemy smites you on one cheek, turn the other because your Daddy Jesus is not asleep. Do you realize how the church operates? My God, you better not take my meekness for weakness! Even when I know you have devoured my name and treated me as 'nothing'. Even when I know of the evils you have spoken about me, I will still be praying for you. I will pray earnestly until tears flow from my eyes. The next time I see you, I will still be able to hug and kiss you because I am a child of God and know that whatever you do to me, you really are doing to yourself.

Remember that the Shekinah glory is the neighbouring spirit and whatever you sow in the body of Christ, you shall surely reap. There are instances when persons within the church operate with a similar spirit with which the scammers operate. They take advantage of your demonstration of God's love and parade through the church, presenting the same material need to a number of believers. Through deception, they receive help from as many as possible for the same need. For example, someone has an electricity bill of seven thousand dollars. That individual requests assistance from as many believers as possible to pay the same bill. Eventually, the sum collected is three or four times the amount needed to settle that one bill.

This person laughs, believing that he has outsmarted the people of God. That is earthly cunning and dirty wisdom! You might even laugh at the people of God you exploited. Note however, that some may have given you all that they had! Know this assuredly! You did not deceive them, you sowed a seed and God will give you a harvest! This is a neighbour word.

"Give to every man that asketh of thee; and of him that taketh away thy goods ask them not again."

Loving and giving, constitutes the foundational principles of the church. Stand on that foundation! Give to him that asks of thee (even when they are scamming). Give them! I told you; do not take the meekness of Gods people for weakness!

Some blatantly live a life of fornication and walk into the church with and unrepentant and presumptuous spirit. In their minds, they are testing the leader's precision in discernment. However, they are totally oblivious that a leader who carries a neighbouring spirit will not seek to expose anyone, unless the Holy Ghost gives that directive. Consequently, they convince themselves that they have fooled the servant of God who chooses to be a leader who covers instead of expose.

In reality, they are actually fooling themselves. You see the church is not run by the leader but by the Holy Ghost. Believers within the body of Christ are in need of breakthroughs. However, only when we behave as children of God can we experience those breakthroughs.

Applying Jesus' teachings to our lives today requires that believers exercise the wisdom which comes from God, whenever they are giving. Whenever you give, you need to give as unto the Lord. If you give with the expectation that the receiver is going to reciprocate, a problem is likely to develop.

You need to be just as careful whenever you lend. God says

> *"But love your enemies, and do good, and lend, hoping for nothing again; and your reward shall be great, and ye shall be the children of the Highest: for He is kind unto the unthankful and to the evil."*

So do not lend what you cannot live without! This is wisdom- a wisdom key! If you lend money which you had set aside to pay your bills and it is not given back on time for you to honour your obligations, you will face financial embarrassment. A problem will then develop between the lender and the borrower.

The one who is unable to repay becomes a slave to the lender and a rift develops within the body of Christ. To avoid this, Jesus admonishes us to lend without expectations. Again, do not lend what you genuinely cannot do without. That way, if the person defaults in repaying, you can lovingly say to him, "It is alright; I am sowing it as a seed in your life. I don't want it back from you."

If you give as unto God, you will avoid disappointment and anger when the commitment to repay is not honoured. This releases the borrower, because while the bible teaches that the borrower is a slave to the lender, it also says that in the kingdom of God, there are no slaves. In the church there are only sons and friends. Do not place yokes upon friends. If you borrow something and are unable to return it, a yoke is upon you and problem develops within the body of Christ.

Jesus also said: *"And as you would that men should do to you, do ye also to them likewise."* Simply put, whatever you want me to do for you or to you; that is what you should do to me and for me.

Pay keen attention to this very important kingdom principle for adherence to it is what differentiates the body of Christ from every other group. Jesus asked the following three questions, which I consider very important in provoking constant self-examination:

For if ye love them which love you, what thank have ye? For the sinners also love those that love them.

And if ye do good to them which do good to you, what thank have ye? For sinners also do even the same.

And if ye lend to them of whom ye hope to receive, what thank have ye? For sinners also lend to sinners, to receive as much again. Luke 6:32-34.

This partially explains why the church is heavily criticized by the world. There are many unbelievers who are given to charity and hospitality. By these characteristics they have established their own righteousness, when comparing themselves with unloving and uncaring believers.

The indwelling of the neighbouring spirit should transform us into extraordinary believers. We must be a cut above the rest! For this reason, I constantly admonish you to consider any act of kindness that you do as this is a seed being sown into the kingdom of God. God is a God of reciprocity! In reciprocating, He opens the hearts of people to bless you. Many times these are complete strangers!

Neither should your motive for giving be to gain recognition. Do not publicize your acts of kindness. Have you ever heard people testifying in church of the things they have done for others? Others too, share the information with those in their circle of friends. Whichever way it is done, God is not pleased. He says in Matthew 6:1-4:

Take heed that ye do not your alms before men. To be seen of them: otherwise ye have no reward of your Father which is in heaven.

Therefore when thou doest thine alms, do not sound a trumpet before thee, as the hypocrites do in the synagogues and in the streets, that they may have glory of men. Verily I say unto you, They have their reward.

But when thou doest alms, let not thy left hand know what thy right hand doeth:

That thine alms may be in secret: and thy Father which seeth in secret Himself shall reward thee openly.

There is also the tendency to consider persons as being ungrateful if they do not publicly declare the act of kindness which was done to them. This is not to be so in the body of Christ. Love, demonstrated through God's way of giving, is done in secret. God sees in secret but rewards us publicly or openly. Whenever you receive your desired applaud from men; that is all you will receive for your giving. Why settle for so little?

God wants to give you a harvest for your giving! If you truly desire God's blessing, do not let your right hand know what your left hand does. Many believers only consider statements like 'The Lord is my shepherd, I shall not want' to be great words from the Lord. However, I implore everyone to walk with the word being released throughout this book. Indeed, obedience to God's instructions will guarantee that He will be our Shepherd as well as our Neighbour. That's the ultimate guarantee that we shall lack no good thing!

Just do good! Do good and also love those who you perceive to hate you. This qualifies you to be called children of the Most High God. This is the line of demarcation between generous folks and those who are a part of the body of Christ. They are filled with the neighbouring spirit.

If you abide by these principles, God will open the windows of heaven and give you a great reward! Great will be your reward from your Father. He is kind even to the unthankful and evil. Those who are atheists- believing that God does not exist- and those who curse God are still beneficiaries of God's goodness and mercies daily. Through His creation, they enjoy God's providence. They also receive a harvest whenever they plant.

If God provides for those who reject Him because He is love, how much more will He take care of His own children? Therefore, as your Father is merciful, be merciful also. Did you get that? Be merciful! The neighbouring spirit does not give up and write-off others who have done wrong. Our Father gives mercy and so should we. We are alive today because His mercies towards us are renewed daily. Truthfully, without that, we would have died a long time ago.

Jesus continued to teach His followers what they needed to do to identify with Him and to be a part of the new movement which He was about to usher in. He said to them: *Judge not, and ye shall not be judged: condemn not, and ye shall not be condemned: forgive, and ye shall be forgiven.* If you have been observing each instruction, you would realize that it had to do with interpersonal relationships; how mankind treats their fellowman. But notice that each action had a predictable consequence that was predetermined by our Heavenly Father.

I do not believe that I am the only one who has concluded that the church is the most judgmental group on planet earth. People in the church judge each other without even establishing the validity of any information they receive. This should be the opposite because the word of God says that charity proveth all things.

The consequence of judging is that you will be judged in the same manner that you judged your neighbour. Jesus was, and is still speaking to the body of Christ. Do not write-off your neighbour even if they have erred!

Many believers are being blocked by evil words that were released over their lives. Today, I want you to place your sanctified hand upon yourself and declare Isaiah 54:17 over your life.

No weapon that is formed against thee shall prosper; and every tongue that rise against thee in judgment thou shalt

condemn. This is the heritage of the servants of the LORD,
and their righteousness is of me, saith the LORD.

All the judgmental tongues that do not want you to be successful in life, I pull them down!

All the 'crab in barrel mentality' tongues, I pull them down!

All wicked tongues, I pull them down!

All condemning tongues, I pull them down!

Every tongue that rises against me in judgment, I condemn now!

Every tongue that rises against you in judgment, I condemn now!

I condemn every judgmental and negative curse word released over our lives; I pull them down!

Every tongue that has arisen against my neighbour, I pull down now in the name of Jesus!

'Forgive and ye shall be forgiven' is probably the most ignored instruction from Jesus. Many carry a spirit of revenge - always hoping for evil to befall their brothers and sisters. Yet it is so important to forgive in order to live a victorious and blessed life in Christ. The Spirit of God constantly reveals to believers who are seeking to get into His presence, who they need to release for the Shekinah Glory to flow in their lives.

Unforgiveness is a direct block to your own forgiveness as well as the free flow of the Spirit of God. My God! If we could only realize how much sickness, spiritual lethargy and unfruitfulness are directly associated with our unwillingness to forgive one another. We would be eager to resolve any misunderstandings among our brethren before hatred, bitterness and animosity take root.

It simply blows my mind as a child of God and a leader in the body of Christ to see how many professing Christians live in malice. I mean from the pulpit to the pew! In some instances for years too! Oh my God! Believers it is time to release each other so the body of Christ can rise to a new dimension in Christ. We must do in excess of what the sinners do; we are called to be a cut above the rest. I told you that I am delivering the word that I have received for the body of Christ in this season: FORGIVE! FORGIVE! FORGIVE!

Now it is up to you, if you want God to forgive you. Remember that the prerequisite is that you first forgive the one who wronged you. Whether it has been a day, month, year, years or decades-FORGIVE! I know that you lay in your bed sometimes and reflect on what was done to you. I know it is so painful that you water your bed with tears. I know that it is so humiliating and you do not want anyone to know what was done to you. But yes! You still have to forgive! It is not for the aggressor or perpetrator, it is for you. Believe me; I can relate to the private pain, even though our circumstances may be different. But I forgave and so can you!

I must hasten to say that the weight that you are going to be relieved of will be worth it! However, there are also many other benefits. There is health and prosperity for your body, soul and spirit. There is no moment greater than this, to stop whatever you are doing, and release yourself by forgiving anyone who has wronged you.

FORGIVE! FORGIVE! FORGIVE! Say, "Lord I forgive ………….. (say the name of the person who you are in malice with).

God wants oneness in the church. He wants the church to be in one accord. Let your neighbour know, "If I have wronged you, please forgive me." Our common enemy-the devil- is so cunning! Whenever he wants to block the flow of the Spirit of God among the believers, he concocts and schemes to sow discord among believers. I am amazed at some of the simple things that he uses to interfere with the fellowship that believers ought to share.

The devil will sometimes place a lie in the mind of a believer that another believer hates them. In the meantime, he arranges an incident that he can use to let the believer whom he told the lie say they have proof of the lie. He sometimes tell both believers the same lie and both end up believing. A seed of bitterness is planted in the hearts of the believers simply because the devil is trying to block their blessings.

Sometimes unawares, a believer goes by without greeting another as a result of preoccupation with personal challenges. Immediately the enemy uses that to substantiate his claim that the believer does not like the other believer. It is farthest from the truth! In fact, had that person who believed that they were ignored really known what the other was going through, they would have instead tried reaching them.

The truth is that those who remain in unforgiveness, do not really touch God with their praise. Even the loudest hallelujah, coming from a heart filled with hate and unforgiveness, is not able to pass the unclean spirits in the second heavens.

You may at times wonder, after having been in the church so long, how comes there is no seemingly forthcoming breakthrough in your life, while others receive major breakthroughs after only six months in the church. You complain that nothing is happening for you, while giftings, callings, houses, cars, healings and deliverances are being released all around you. Do you really want to know why?

Check your heart! God says that you have to guard your heart with all diligence. You must be careful because the devil wants to block your blessing. If he can put evil thoughts in your heart, then you will not be able to flow in the Spirit of God; your heart will be clogged. The bible tells us that out of our hearts flow the issues of life.

You must constantly search your heart to identify any root of bitterness that may be springing up in you. The moment you realize that someone is being held up in your heart, you must forgive and release them in order to get that breakthrough that you have so desperately been praying and believing for.

I am not throwing words! I am trying to help you my beloved neighbour!

Finally, Jesus said to His followers,

> *"Give and it shall be given unto you; good measure,*
> *pressed down, and shaken together, and running over, shall*

men give into your bosom. For with the same measure that
ye mete withal it shall be measured to you again."

The Spirit of God wants to dwell in your praise. For this to happen, God says, "GIVE!" You should be a house of seed; a basket; a storehouse; a warehouse of seeds. Wherever you go, you should plant seeds. My good neighbour, you must be a giver; a sower! Yes, GIVE!

In fact, Jesus is actually saying that if you give judgment, you shall receive judgment. If you give forgiveness, you shall receive forgiveness. Whatever you give to your neighbour; that is what you will receive. If you sow love, God will release love from people into your life. The principle is simple, but profound: Give and it shall be given back to you.

I wrap this message up with this fundamental principle: *Give and it shall be given back to you; good measure, pressed down, shaken together and running over shall MEN give into your bosom.* I have placed 'MEN' in blocks for emphasis. Contrary to the expectations of some believers, the neighbouring spirit works through men.

When the Holy Ghost came, it fell on men, making us God's ambassadors in the earth realm. So whatever you do to men, God is going to do to you. I think by now you realize why it is so important to carefully monitor our interpersonal relationships. We are wise when we treat others well. Do you want God to raise you up? Just begin to do good!

The word from Jesus Himself is, *"For with the same measure that ye mete withal it shall be measured to you again."* The word 'mete' is synonymous to measure. In the kingdom of God, there is reciprocity in giving. However, God determines how much and what you will be given in return. He also opens the way for the reward to be delivered through men.

Love is the key to your breakthrough my neighbour!

Finally, I am deliberately provoking you to godliness and goodliness as I no longer refer to you as leaders but now as neighbours; my good neighbours. It is my prayer that the neighbouring spirit infiltrate the life of every reader so that you can be elevated by God. Always remember that if your desire is that God will raise you up, you must begin to love. If you love each other, you will cover each other.

Love begins with loving yourself and then loving those in your house. You will not be able to love the people at your workplace, if you do not love those within your own home. If you cannot love at your workplace, neither will you be able to love within the church. However, your home is the foundation!

Receiving from God, begins with your household. That is the first training ground! Get it right at home and you will get it right in the other environments where you interact with people. Treat the people in your immediate family well. Forgive them whenever they wrong you. Live peaceably with them as much as is possible and let the neighbouring spirit indwell your home.

Neighbour, my good neighbour, Jesus told me to tell you that 'Love is the key!' Although in church, you run the aisles and speak in tongues at ninety nine miles per hour; if you gather and speak ill of the elder, missionary and chorister, you are in trouble with God! You ran the aisle in vain!

Without the key, you cannot unlock the blessings of God. Charity, of which we spoke earlier, is the love that gives unconditionally; no strings attached. It gives without expectations for reciprocity. If you only love to preach, sing, dance and manifest the gifts without charity, all is useless! Without charity, all of these dramatic displays are described in God's word as sounding brass and tinkling cymbals.

My preaching, in the absence of charity is meaningless! Prophesy from now until next week; know all the secrets in the bible but have no love; you are nothing! If you have faith which can move mountains, you are still required to love me, if you want to go to the next level.

You must love me! You must suffer with me! And suffer long too; I know! I know! That thought is painful, but suffer with me, you must; for love suffers long. Love is kind. So you cannot proclaim that you are walking in the spirit and be so 'stingy.' In Jamaican dialect, 'mean like star-apple.'

You might be in the company of other believers and have a few thousand dollars in your possession. You realize that one of your neighbours is really hungry but you refuse to offer him even a drink. That is not God-like! Be a giver, if you want God to open doors that no man can shut!

This has been said in numerous ways throughout this book, and at the risk of sounding redundant, I choose to repeat it. I think that the purpose God has for me to write this book is defeated if you fail to realize that love truly covers all! My mission would not be accomplished if you read this book to the end without experiencing the transforming power of God through love! I would consider myself as having failed to effectively deliver God's word to inspire change within the body of Christ that will ultimately spread like wildfire to those without.

After all that has been said, the message in a nutshell is one word: LOVE! Love does not envy. Neither does it stand before the mirror, adorning itself with the intention of entering the house of God to boast on others; making fashion statements that no one can dress as well as you. Instead, love looks at an item of clothing admiringly but gladly and lovingly identifies a neighbour whose appearance would be greatly enhanced if they were blessed with it. That is love!

Love does not exalt itself; it is not puffed up; does not discriminate; is not partial. It does not divide the body of Christ but rather unites. Some in the church select friends only from among those who belong to the upper echelon of society. To these elitist folks, those who do menial jobs are considered 'nobody'. These are expected to consider themselves privileged when they are acknowledged with a 'cold' greeting.

The neighbouring spirit, however, does not tolerate partiality within the body of Christ. It searches and is drawn to loving those who appear to be insignificant. They are the ones who the neighbouring spirit will reach, without ignoring others. Those who are rejected because they are poor in material things should be esteemed among us in the body of Christ.

Some believers are embarrassed to be identified with their brethren whenever they are among their 'upper class' friends. Neighbour, if you are real and have charity, you would not consider it humiliating to be seen on the television or social media worshipping with your fellow brethren.

Neighbour, I just want to remind you of the example set by Jesus in recruiting the twelve disciples. These were selected and trained by Him; then commissioned immediately before His departure from earth, to continue the new movement He gave His life to establish. His neighbouring spirit ruled out isms, schisms and partiality.

There was no favouritism! He stepped over the educated, the Jews, the Pharisees, the Priests and the Sanhedrin Counsel. He went down to the Sea of Galilee and chose Matthew the thief, the sons of Zebedee, the uneducated Peter and the others we have read of. He knew all of them inside and out. He is God! So He knew their most private thoughts. Yet He chose them and covered them with His love. He never exposed them to the enemies but rebuked them privately if necessary. Yes! Believers' behaviour sometimes necessitates that we get a little whipping to keep on ticking! His love required that He chastened them but He always covered them.

The church does not operate by man's wisdom and man-made rules. The church is not run by education, even though it is good as part of our preparation to function in this world's system. The church is run by the HOLY GHOST! It requires that every believer in the body of Christ, humbles himself and operate in accordance with the principles laid out in the last words of Jesus.

Wash each other's feet so that the Spirit of God will indwell you. If you can wash each other's feet; if you can cover each other, then you are a candidate to experience the move of God in this season. Are you ready?

Just forget about yourself and open your spirit to be touched with the problems and pains of your neighbour. If you want God to use you; if you want the gifts of God to manifest in your life, then you must understand this key principle. Jesus told Moses that the garment which is to be made for the High Priest should have alternating pomegranates and bells at the hem.

Bible history informs us that a rope had to be tied around the ankle of the High Priest before he enters the Holy of Holies to offer the yearly sacrifice for the children of God. No one else is allowed to enter the Most Holy Place. Everyone else had to await his return on the outside. Should the sacrifice he presents be unacceptable to God, he would be struck dead in the Holy of Holies.

This moment was, therefore, one of anxiety and great anticipation. They could only know if the High Priest was still alive by listening for the chiming of the bells as he ministered before the Lord. If there was no sound forthcoming, an indication that the priest had been struck dead by God, no one could enter to retrieve the body. Anyone who dared to enter would receive a similar fate. The rope which is attached to his ankle would be used to pull his lifeless body from the Holy of Holies.

God's instruction was to place a fruit between each bell so that there would be a soft, harmonious sound instead of a clanging sound. He said to me: Son, the bell represents the fruit of the Spirit. Those who are on the outside of the body of Christ cannot know which church Jesus the High Priest is in, without the bells and fruit. It is the gifts in operation which allow them to realize that the High Priest is present in the church.

However, the fruit between each pair of bells is quite symbolic. Jesus said that the way in which the world will be able to identify His disciples will be by the agape love that is expressed in their interactions with each other. To love each other unconditionally is to manifest the love of Jesus Christ.

God says, "Son, it is time for the church to take to the streets! It is time for the church to bring the glory to those on the outside! We are living in the final moments of time! The coming of Christ is closer than ever before. God is doing a quick work! He has fast-forwarded His mandate. This is the final moment! Church of Jesus Christ, GET READY!!!

Are you ready to go out? Are you really ready to go out? If you answered in the affirmative, then it is also time, having forgiven everyone to shout, GLORY! As you do, open your spirit so that the Shekinah Glory, the neighbouring spirit will come down and abide with you. This is the spirit which prepares you to impact your world for Jesus.

As we war those unclean spirits blocking them from accepting the gospel so they can become joint heirs in the kingdom of God; we also need to demonstrate the unconditional love of Jesus that covers. Together we will receive the manifold blessings which God had for us before the foundation of the world. We need to fulfill God's divine will for our lives.

Get ready my neighbour! Be a leader who covers and watch God use you to transform this nation as you cover it with the Agape Love. Let the love of God flow! If you wronged anyone, make it right! Love! If anyone wronged you, release them! Love! Let the agape – unconditional love flow!

I feel God wants His glory to flow through His people today to a lost and dying world. Now is the time to surrender all to God and let the neighbouring spirit, the Shekinah glory flow. Let it flow among His people; uniting our hearts; breaking down the walls of segregation and destroying all the isms and schisms within the body of Christ. Hallelujah!

Let it flow, releasing 'dunamis' that breaks yokes; sets captives free; raises the dead; heals the sick; breaks curses and ushers His people into the blessings that He so badly wants to release in our lives in these last days. Glory!

Let me go please, if I have wronged you! I need the Shekinah glory to flow in my life. I want to go to a new dimension! Many come to the church because they are sick; do not block their healing! Someone is under pressure; do not block their breakthrough! God wants to show up in the church! Get rid of the isms and schisms!

The Holy Ghost has released some angels with an assignment to visit the churches with brooms. They have been instructed to sweep out some stuff- from the pulpit to the pew. A fresh wind is blowing! Neighbour can you feel it?

Sweep Holy Ghost! Sweep out the demon of division!

Sweep Holy Ghost! Sweep out the spirit of un-forgivenes!

Sweep Holy Ghost! Sweep out the demon of bitterness!

Sweep Holy Ghost! Sweeeeeeeeeeeeeeeep! Sweep out the demon of hatred!

Sweep Holy Ghost! Sweep out back biting!

Sweep Holy Ghost! Sweep out strife!

Sweep Holy Ghost! Sweep! Sweep! Sweep! Sweep! From the pulpit to the pew! Sweep!!!!!!!!

It is time to connect! It is time to hold on to your neighbour! Hallelujah!

Let it flow! Let it flow!

It is time to go to a new dimension in the kingdom of God. Love will take you there! A leader who covers is a leader who has risen to a new dimension in the kingdom of God.

Welcome to this new dimension!

PRAYER

Oh Great I Am that I am; God of Abraham; God of Isaac; Great God of Jacob, here we are in your presence today, presenting ourselves to you – the temple which you desire to indwell.

We ask you now to speak to Your church, the ecclesia; the called out ones to whom you have spoken through this tool. Lord I have delivered that which you have placed in my spirit to deliver to Your people.

Lord, please unctionize Your people, that we will not merely function in the physical realm, but function by divine inspiration. Father, one more time, we come against all diabolical forces. We come against all hindering spirits, against all demonic powers, positioning themselves to block the will of God from being fulfilled. We render them powerless.

Arise Oh God and let our enemies be scattered!

We speak to every contrary wind!

We break every curse!

We pull down every stronghold!

We come against every spirit that comes against the will of God!

Father in the name of Jesus, give high ranking angels charge. Let them burn unclean spirits with the fire of God.

Father we claim victory in the lives of Your people and in the church. Victory belongs to the church.

Let the blood of Jesus flow! Let it flow Oh God like hot lava! Let the fire of God burn! Let liquid fire fall among Your people.

God we thank You for victory that is in Your efficacious blood. Your supreme blood, Oh Jesus Christ flows today.

Oh Holy Spirit we thank you for victory in Jesus name. Hallelujah!

Throw your hand in the air and echo the blood of Jesus! Blood! Blood! Blood!

The blood of Jesus prevails! The blood of Jesus prevails! Hallelujah!

We overcome by the blood! Hallelujah! We overcome by the blood of Jesus! Hallelujah!

The blood of Jesus! The blood of Jesus! The blood of Jesus! Hallelujah!

Go ahead and praise God for the victory as a leader who covers! Hallelujah!

Welcome to this new dimension leader who covers!

About the Author

From the author of "Warring Unclean Spirits" comes "The Leader Who Covers." Apostle Winston Baker, a dynamic preacher and devout father of six beautiful children whom are also a part of the body of Christ, continues to allow God to use him in delivering the kingdom message to His people. He has been saved, sanctified and filled with the Holy Ghost for over twenty years. On him, God has placed an extra-ordinary anointing and gifting by the Holy Ghost and there is no denying that many signs and wonders have been wrought through him.

With humility and holiness, Apostle Baker follows the guidance of the Holy Spirit as he displays the truth about God. He currently spearheads the King Jesus Pentecostal Fellowship; a vibrant and fast growing ministry second to none in this season. In his Ministry, the lame walks, the blind sees, the dumb speaks, HIV/AIDS and Cancer healed and the demon possessed set free; as there is no refutation that Satan acted ultra-vires and was thrown out of heaven; and that since then he has been trying to wreak havoc on the lives of God's people by diverting their attention from the truth about salvation.

Apostle Baker is a tested, tried and proven under-shepherd whose vehement mission is the winning of souls for the kingdom of heaven and the waging of war against the kingdom of darkness.

He is a true and powerful man of God, chosen for such a time as this.

Jay Janette
566-7471

CPSIA information can be obtained
at www.ICGtesting.com
Printed in the USA
FFOW03n0405100118
44340031-43999FF

9 781506 905259